To Francis

Congratulations on your 70TH 16·4·98

from Pat and Mother.

Hastings Past

The sands and pier from the *Queen's Hotel*, *c.*1900.

Hastings Past

Rex Marchant

Phillimore

1997

Published by
PHILLIMORE & CO. LTD.
Shopwyke Manor Barn, Chichester, West Sussex

ISBN 1 86077 046 0

Printed and bound in Great Britain by
BIDDLES LTD.
Guildford, Surrey

To My Sally

Contents

List of Illustrations

Frontispiece: Hastings seafront from the *Queen's Hotel*, *c*.1900

Acknowledgements

My thanks are due to the many people who have shown a helpful interest in this book and have come foward with information and illustrations. I have not been able to use all the material that they provided me with, but nonetheless I am very grateful for their kindness. My particular thanks go to the staff of the Hastings Museum and the members of the Hastings Modern History Workshop, who have been most generous with their help and with the loan of illustrations. Above all, though, my thanks go to my wife, Sally, who has not only given me wholehearted support and encouragement but has saved me so much time through undertaking so much of the necessary clerical work.

Illustration Acknowledgements

Ron Fellows, 86, 127, 136; Mr. Mills, 147; David Padgham, 24, 28, 48, 52, 78, 93, 103, 105, 114, 115, 132, 140, 143, 149, 152; Miss Joan Robins, 40, 96, 107, 137; Jeanne Smythe, 15, 21, 29, 49, 69, 75-7, 108, 130, 141, 144; Miss A. Spicer, 46. All other illustrations are from the author's own collection.

Chapter One

1066–And Much More

HASTINGS prompts a conditioned reflex; say it and the response will almost always be '1066' or 'That's where the battle was fought'. It is always *the* battle. Of all the battles fought in this country's 2,000 years of recorded history, the Battle of Hastings remains unique, the one that virtually everyone knows about and the only one to which most people can put the correct date. It looms large in the national consciousness and inevitably dominates local historical awareness, so much so that it can appear to be both the beginning and the end of the Hastings story; it blocks the view of everything that came before it and its shadow obscures all that has happened since.

However, the history of Hastings comprises more than just the battle. The story of the town began 1,000 years or more before the Norman Conquest, and in the 900 and more years since it has continued to be full of incident and interest. To future

1 It is likely that there was a castle of some sort here long before 1066. Legend says that the original builders, undecided which hill to put it on, released a falcon at sunrise and watched where it flew. It swooped towards the West Hill, so that is where they put the castle.

generations, 1924 may be as important a Hastings date as 1066; 1924 being the year when John Logie Baird sent the flickering image of a Maltese Cross from a transmitter in one part of his Hastings workshop to a receiver a few feet distant in the world's first successful demonstration of television. William the Conqueror and John Logie Baird both changed the future, and they both did it at Hastings.

But what about the claim that the town's story began so long before the Conquest? It has been previously suggested that the first settlement in the area was not until A.D. 893, when a Danish raider named Haesta or Hasten landed here. However, this must be wrong since there are references to the town that predate this. The *Historia Regum* of Simeon of Durham states plainly that in A.D. 771, 'Offa, King of the Mercians, subdued the people of Hastings by force of arms', and there is another reference in a document of Offa's reign to 'the port of Hastingas'.

It has even been suggested that the name dates back to the fifth century when 'The Hastings, the noblest race of the Goths' supposedly took over an abandoned Roman town and made it their capital.[1] That is romanticised conjecture but the dating certainly seems likely. The south-east was settled very early by the post-Roman invaders and on the continent a place name containing the equivalent of '-ingas' is seen as indicative of a Germanic settlement of the fifth or sixth centuries.

The Saxon Aelle and his three sons attacked Sussex and founded the kingdom of the South Saxons in A.D. 477 but some years prior to that the Britons had hired Jutes to help fight off other enemies, which had resulted in a very early Jutish colony being established in Kent. The balance of probability puts the Hastingas among those Jutish mercenaries; it has to be significant that Hastings was the only non-Saxon settlement in Sussex.

Nor was it regarded as a part of Sussex until much later. All early references make it clear that it was separate and independent from both Sussex and Kent. It could well be that the ninth-century Haesten hailed from the same ancestral homeland north of the Elbe, hence the confusion of names. In any case, the argument is only about when the town received its name not about when it became a centre of population, because that long predates the arrival of the Hastingas.

The existence of a Roman town must remain conjectural but it seems very likely. A strong case has been advanced for it having been Novus Portus, a town mentioned in the records but the location of which has never been conclusively identified. Hastings–it is convenient to use its modern name–would have been ideally situated to provide port facilities for the iron producing sites which the Romans established in its immediate hinterland. It is also in just the right place to fill what would otherwise have been a gap in the fortifications set up around the south-eastern coasts. That it was generally referred to in Saxon times as Hastingaceastre has been taken by some as supporting evidence for there having been a Roman town.

Be that as it may, it is unarguable that it was already a centre of population when the Romans arrived and had been for a long time. Some of the local caves have revealed traces of occupancy going back far into prehistory and finds of flint arrowheads and Bronze-Age artifacts show that it remained a favoured location over thousands of years. Certainly there was a large settlement here by the time Caesar mounted his expedition against Britain in 55 B.C. The Iron-Age promontory forts on the East and West Hills prove that and represent a considerable investment of time and labour by a relatively large population over a long period.

In 1990, the county archaeologist described the East Hill fort as 'one of the best preserved and most impressive earthworks in East Sussex'. The entrance fosse has been cut out of solid rock to a depth of 7-8 feet and a huge embankment, still 20 feet high in places, ran 300 yards north and south along the crest of the hill, the material for it having come from a wide trench cut

2 St Clement's Caves were exploited in the late 18th and 19th centuries as a source of good quality sand but are otherwise of little historical interest. However, other local caves have yielded evidence of human occupation far back in prehistory.

out from the rock. Further earthworks ran parallel and at right angles to this main embankment.

Caesar has left an account of a place which he attacked where a narrow inlet of the sea was shut in by heights from which weapons and rocks were hurled down on those below; this description, allied to the existence of the forts, suggests that it could have been Hastings. It is also possible that boats from the town were in the 200-strong fleet with which the Veneti and their allies attacked Caesar's ships in 56 B.C. It is known that there were British boats in this fleet and it is also known, again from Caesar, that the iron found near the British coast was exported in exchange for copper and other goods. With iron so plentiful locally and with a suitable inlet directly under its fort, Hastings was ideally situated to be the entrepot for this trade and so to have boats available to send out against a common foe.

When the conquest of Britain was completed in the first century, the Romans immediately started the exploitation of local iron and soon half a dozen sites were being worked in the immediate locality. The one at Beauport Park was probably the most productive in the whole of Britain and one of the largest in Roman Empire. Even the waste from these iron workings, the slag, was economically important, being valued as ideal material for road metalling.

The iron-working sites employed a lot of people. After an enlargement *c.*A.D. 200, Beauport Park alone is reckoned to have accounted for 1,000 men. When the workers at the other sites are added, and the administrative superstructure, the ancillary services, tradesmen, camp followers and families, it comes to an impressive total, the more so given that Silchester, an important regional centre, is credited with an adult population of only 2,500.

There must have been an urban centre somewhere and the obvious place is Hastings. Even if the Beauport Park complex was self-sufficient, there would have been out-dwellers and so the established settlement at Hastings would inevitable have grown during the Roman occupation. Nor is the absence of remains of that period any argument against this. Nothing, apart from the most impressive Beauport bath-house, described as 'one of the finest surviving Roman buildings in southern England',[2] has been found anywhere in the district. Had the harbour for the export of the iron been at Sedlescombe, as some believe, one would have expected traces of it to have been discovered. At Hastings there is an obvious explanation for this lack–coastal erosion. If anything is left of the Roman town it has long been under the sea.

The process of erosion and inundation, well attested to from the medieval period onwards, would have been operating in Roman times as well. It and periodic violent storms have caused known dramatic changes to the coastline. There is also the phenomenon of the eastward drift of shingle, which has alternately created and destroyed anchorages as the shingle first piled up against the western side of a promontory or line of rocks and then either spilled over or was swept round to fill the harbour that it had previously created. The combined effect has been to make the coastline transitory and, if further proof were needed that great areas of previously dry land are now under water, it is provided by the submarine forest that stretches the length of Hastings and beyond. Several incarnations of Hastings have been drowned, and Novus Portus could well be one of them.

Such a drowning could even explain the closure and abandonment of the Beauport iron-workings midway through the third century, only about forty years after they had been enlarged. Alternatively, they could have become too vulnerable to sea raiders, including perhaps the Hastingas who were later to settle here. There is evidence from various sites in southern England of violent upheavals in the third century, with villages and villas attacked and destroyed.

3 Maps of the ancient coastline can only be conjectural but photographs such as this illustrate the constant process of change. Since the Ordnance Survey of 1871-2 the cliffs have retreated by up to 80 metres in some sections. Both Lovers' Seat and this group of Coastguard buildings have been lost in recent years.

4 The beaches provide a clear illustration of the effects of the eastward drift. Shingle piles against the groynes, creating miniature bays on their eastern sides. Before Galley Hill and White Rock were eroded, they acted like giant groynes and the bays thus formed were deepened and scoured by the Asten and the Priory streams.

Whatever the reason, the Romans left Beauport. The copper tanks, lead pipes, window glass and even some of the roof tiles of the bath-house were removed and the shell of the building and about 100,000 tons of slag were left, soon to be forgotten and to remain so until 1868, when local road-makers began to quarry the slag. The bath-house itself was not rediscovered until 1969.

Although no Roman buildings have been discovered actually in Hastings, there have been sufficient finds of coins and other objects to support the view that it housed a considerable Romano-British population. One hoard was found in 1840 on the East Hill in the area known as St George's Churchyard, traditionally the site of a Roman fort. The coins, all brass, consisted of two collections, one from the second century A.D. and the other from the fourth. Another hoard of over 50 coins was literally turned up in the 1860s when foundations were being dug for the houses in Warrior Square.

Smaller finds have also been made at various locations, from Ore through to St Leonards Gardens and Albany Road, with a cluster of finds in the Silverhill area–at Clarence Road, Beaufort Road and Vale Road. Coins have also been found occasionally on the beach, which possibly supports the theory that there is a drowned Novus Portus somewhere off-shore. The most exciting discovery, though, was made in 1989 at a site in Elphinstone Road. First 92 bronze coins were found, along with the remains of a locally-made pot in which they had apparently been buried, and then, about forty feet away, a collection of 52 silver denarii. A further seven denarii were found a little later.

Interestingly, this Elphinstone Road find was not the result of a lucky scan with a metal detector; the scan was undertaken deliberately because the searchers believed that the area was occupied in Roman times.

It is probable that a remnant of the Romano-British population was still in the area when the Hastingas arrived, but what then happened to it and the exact date of that arrival will probably never be known. What is known, though, is that the newcomers founded an independent mini-state that kept its separate identity until well into the Middle Ages. As late as A.D. 1011, the Anglo-Saxon Chronicle, recording the onslaughts of the Danes, described how they had 'harried our wretched people in Kent, Sussex and Hastings', thus emphasising the area's distinct identity.

It is likely that the Hastingas landed and had their original settlement at the extreme western end of the present town, in the Bulverhythe and Pebsham area. As the 19th-century Sussex historian M.A. Lower pointed out,[3] the similarity between the name of the river at that end of the town, the Asten, and that of the town itself is probably not coincidental. Another telling point is that the place of execution long remained in that area, felons being drowned near Bulverhythe in a stream called Storthisdale.

By the end of the Saxon period, Hastings had moved eastward, but still not so far as Old Town. The indications are that the Hastings in which William the Conqueror set up his headquarters in 1066 was not far from the present town centre, and that the harbour was protected by the White Rock headland, which then jutted out into the sea more or less opposite the junction of Claremont and Robertson Street with the Sea Front.

Another pointer to the site of the Saxon township is that the church of St Michael stood on the White Rock cliff in the region of Prospect Place and White Rock Gardens. St Michael is the patron saint of the town and it is he who appears on the town seal. Clearly, the church dedicated to him would be the principal one in the town, which would cluster about it.

There is reason to believe that William

5 *Left.* The town seal dates from *c.*1300 and since it depicts a naval action with the Cinque Ports ship trumphant, it could relate to the victory off Sluys in 1296. The reverse shows St Michael killing the dragon.

6 *Below.* The White Rock before its removal.

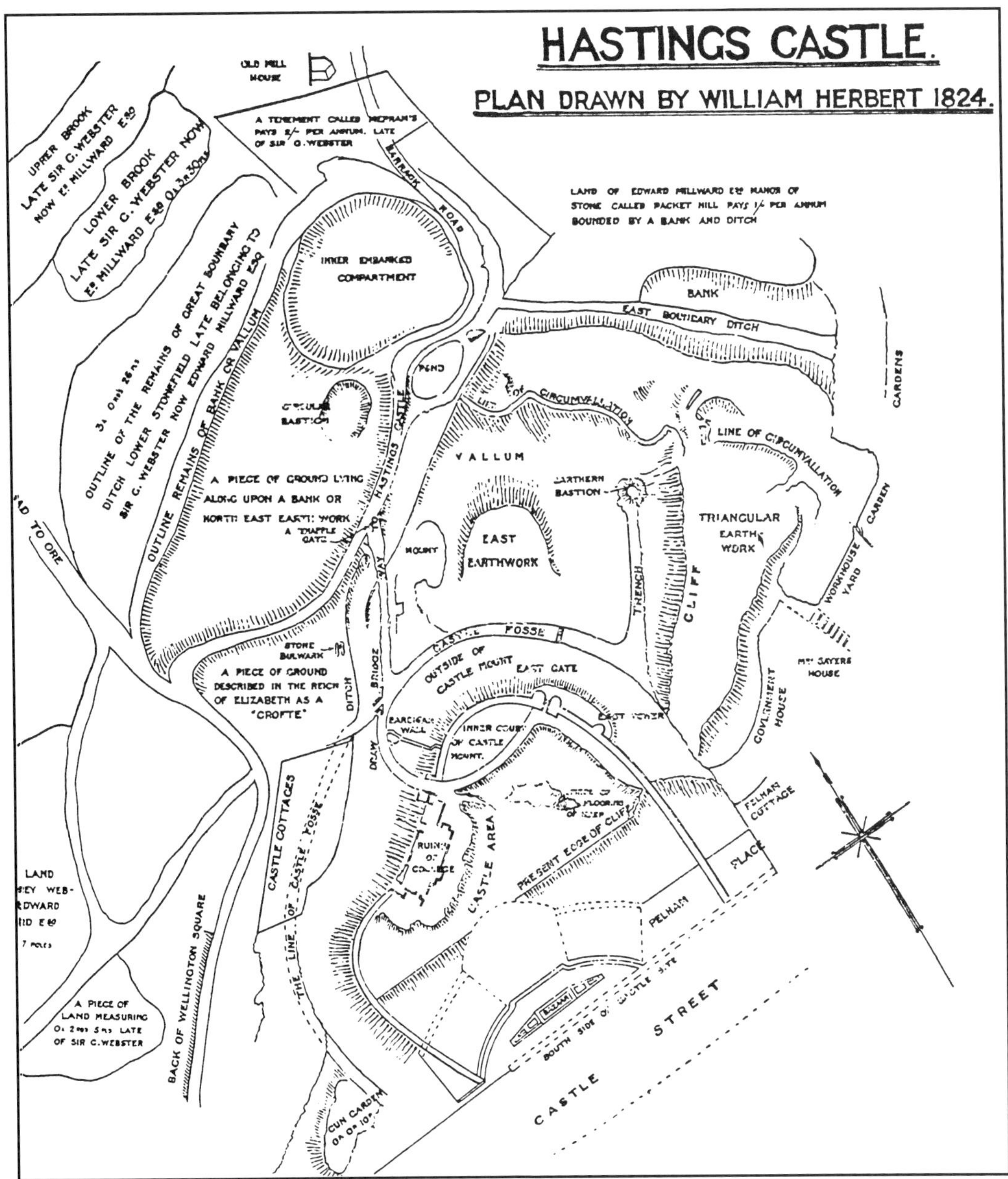

7 This plan shows the extent of the ancient earthworks on the castle site. It also illustrates, as Dawson commented in *Hastings Castle*, the great changes wrought upon the hill since the development of the town of Hastings from a fishing village at the commencement of the 19th century.

made his encampment not on the site of the castle, as is usually assumed, but on the outskirts of this Saxon town, on open ground between the present railway station and Bohemia. The Bayeux Tapestry shows a prefabricated wooden castle being erected but there are also references to a castle being dug, and traces of what were supposed to be his entrenchments were still visible in that region before the railway was built. Incidentally, one historian has declared that on William's ships were carpenters and

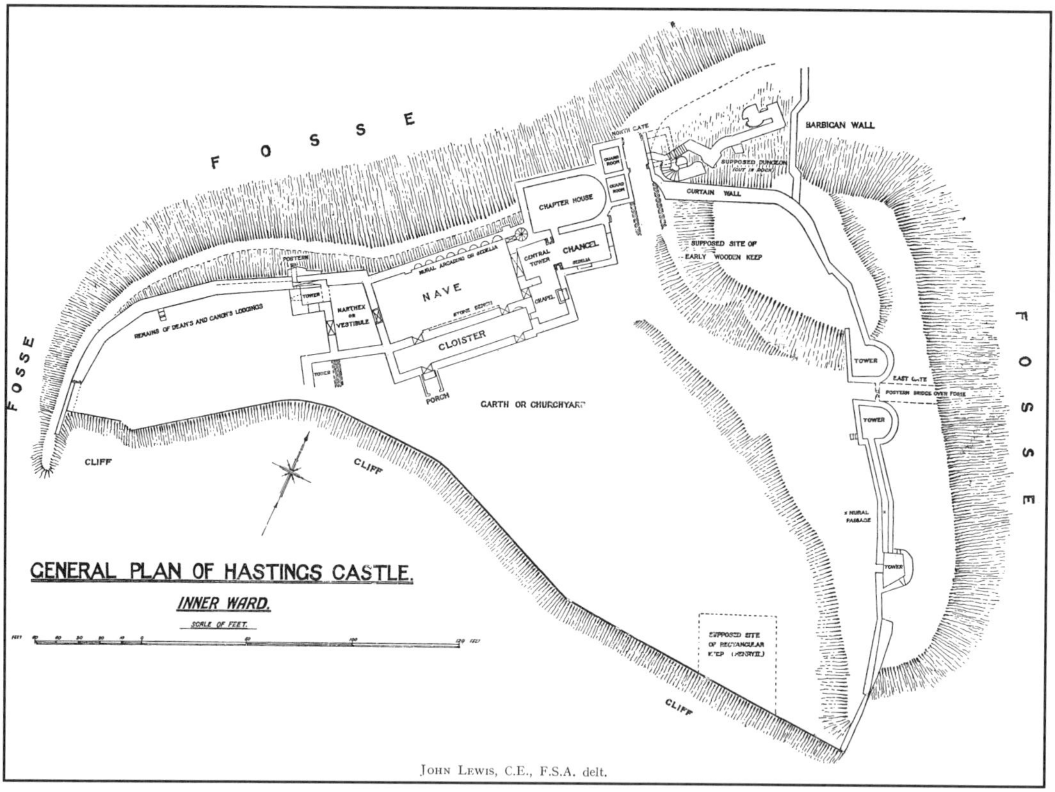

GENERAL PLAN OF HASTINGS CASTLE.

INNER WARD.

JOHN LEWIS, C.E., F.S.A. delt.

8 Plan of the Castle, Inner Ward. The collegiate church was separated from the military part of the castle and included the church itself, the chapter house, cloisters, a solar, a room to receive pilgrims, the deanery house, residences for the prebend, vicars and chaplains, a grammar school and a singing school, stabling and a cemetery and gardens.

9 Before the building of promenades and sea defences, high seas would flood far inland, overwhelming low-lying areas. This photograph was taken in 1929 when the new promenade linking Hastings and St Leonards was being built.

smiths 'who brought on shore 3 wooden castles ready prepared beforehand' and then 'marked out a camp and erected 2 of the wooden castles as receptacles for provisions'.[4]

It seems likely that the fortunes of the town were at a low ebb even before William's arrival, and that one of the periodic natural disasters had destroyed much of the low-lying part of the town beneath the cliffs. There may even have been a cumulative series of disasters–including the ravages of the Danes in 1011 and the floods of 1014, of which the Anglo-Saxon Chronicle said that 'on the eve of St Michael's Mass came the great sea flood wide throughout this land, and run so far up as it never before had done, and washed away many Towns, and a countless number of people'.[5]

One result of all this had been the beginnings of a relocation in the Old Town valley, on the Manor of Rameslie land granted to the Abbey of Fécamp by Cnut at the behest of his wife Emma, who was Norman and patron of the Abbey. This movement would then have been further encouraged by the destruction wrought by William's men. However, an authoritative work on the townships of that period[6] is in no doubt that loss of land to the sea was the main reason for the relocation and puts the founding of 'new' Hastings at *c.*1069.

For some time afterwards, it was referred to as the New Burg [new borough] and the Domesday entry for Rameslie reads:

> 'In this manor is a new Borough; 64 Burgesses pay £8 less 2s; in Hastings 4 burgesses and 14 smallholders pay 63s'.

Two hundred years later, the New Burg itself was 'overthrown and laid waste by the violence and inundation of the sea'.[7] All the southern part of it, including the original St Clement's church, was destroyed and drowned. The church was rebuilt on its present site in 1286 and those who had lost their homes moved to yet another new Hastings, that part of the Old Town that lies to the north of Courthouse Street.

The same storms and floods caused further destruction and depopulation in the St Michael's area, though the church survived for a little longer. It was still included in a list of the town's churches compiled in 1291, but it had disappeared by 1372. Its foundations were rediscovered in 1834, when a coastguard station was being built on St Michael's cliff.

Damage to the harbour, making it difficult to accommodate all his fleet, may have been the reason why William landed at Pevensey–assuming that this is what he did do–instead of sailing directly to Hastings, which he had clearly decided on as his base. Had he simply been blown off course, which has been suggested, this would have been mentioned in at least one of the contemporary accounts of the invasion. In the absence of such a mention, we have to look for a compelling reason for him to have subjected his army, many of the men and horses suffering badly from the effects of the crossing, to the circuitous 26-mile trek to Hastings.

10 This lifeboat house was built in 1882 and demolished in 1956. The first RNLI boat, the *Victoria*, arrived in 1858 but was housed at Rock-a-Nore. Before 1858, the town had its own lifeboat–the *Ariel*, paid for by public subscription after six coastguards lost their lives trying to rescue the crew of the Rye collier, the *Good Intent.*

11 *Above.* The early Hastings lifeboats enjoyed little success but, between 1901 and 1931, the *Charles Arkcol 11* saved 28 lives. Although still powered only by oars and sails, and often needing to be taken to Bo-peep for a safe launching, it managed quicker responses, being crewed by fishermen rather than by coastguards, some of whom had to be fetched from their station at Fairlight.

12 *Left.* The lifeboatmen meeting Princess Elizabeth. These men crewed the *MTC*, successor to the *Cyril* and *Lilian Bishop* that had taken part in the Dunkirk evacuation. The *MTC* was in service between 1950 and 1964, was launched 56 times and credited with saving 55 lives.

If this decision was not forced on him by the deficiencies of the harbour, then it could have been prompted by caution, by the desire to avoid a damaging and possibly disastrous encounter at sea with the 'butse carls' of Hastings. These seem to have been the marine equivalent of the hus-carls, the picked fighting men who formed the king's bodyguard and were the nearest that the Saxons had to a standing army. They had a formidable reputation and could have caused havoc amongst William's over-loaded vessels. By coming into Hastings from the landward side, he avoided them and might even have been able then to prevent them landing at their own home port.

It is tempting to speculate that the 'butse carls', repulsed from Hastings, sailed up the Brede to join with Harold and to fight alongside him in that final desperate battle. Perhaps, though, he sent them back to blockade Hastings, for the near-contemporary historian Ordericus Vitalis wrote that he 'caused a fleet of seventy ships ... to guard the coast' so that the Normans should not escape by sea.

It should be remembered that a large percentage of Harold's depleted army was drawn from the territory of the Hastingas, and the butse carls would have wanted to be involved in some way because they owed a special allegiance to the house of Godwin. In 1052, according to the Anglo-Saxon Chronicle, Earl Godwin had met with 'all the Kentish men and all the butse-carls from Hastings', who had declared that 'with him they would die and live'.

This meeting would seem to have been with the rudimentary Cinque Ports organisation, the five ports–Hastings, Dover, Romney, Hythe and Sandwich–that for centuries provided the kings of England with a navy in return for freedom from taxation and other privileges. Hastings is the only one of the five not in Kent but the special mention of it implies more than a mere geographical distinction. This and other references to the butse carls suggests that they comprised a special elite force and possibly had an agreement to provide ships and men that was earlier than that arrived at with the Cinque Ports as a whole. The Confederacy of the Five Ports was set up in the reign of Edward the Confessor, but there is no reason why it should not have grown out of earlier agreements with individual towns.

A possible date for such an agreement with Hastings is A.D. 928. That was when the town was accorded the right to a mint, which could have been part of the *quid pro quo.* Another possibility is that, after Offa had defeated Hastings in 771, he allowed it to retain some autonomy in return for ship service. An ambiguous statement in a document from later in Offa's reign could be interpreted to support this idea. Various

13 Meeting of the Court of Brotherhood and Guestling in 1962. The 'high courte of Shepway', presided over by the Lord Warden, linked the Cinque Ports to central government, but more domestic matters were administered by the Court of Brotherhood and Guestling. The latter was originally a local court limited to Hastings, Rye and Winchelsea but later merged with the Brotherhood.

lands, including the 'sea-port of Hastings' and a salt works situated there, were supposedly gifted to the French abbey of St Denis and the monks complained about attacks on their workmen by 'the King's men' in the port. These 'king's men' could have been members of a garrison put there by Offa or they could have been Hastingers who had accepted the king's service, forerunners of the butse carls.

Such an early agreement could have been the basis of Hastings' claims to be the premier Cinque Port. However, the authenticity of this 'salt works' document has been questioned, and in the records of the Cinque Ports the only distinction accorded to Hastings is that in its hey-day it was bracketed with Dover as the largest contributor to the combined fleet, each of them providing 21 of the 57 ships demanded of the five ports.

These ships, each with a crew of 21 men, 'strong, apt, well-armed and prepared for the service of the king',[8] were to be available for 15 days. If required for longer, the king then paid them at the daily rate of 3d. for a crew member and 6d. each for the master and the constable. A much higher wage was paid by the Conqueror's successors to those who manned the king's own ship, which was kept at Hastings and was presumably built here. The master of this ship was paid 12d. a day and a payment of £7 10s., almost certainly for the crew, was made each time the ship was used.[9]

William II, better remembered as Rufus, was frequently in Hastings on his way to and from France and in 1090 summoned his barons and bishops to the town to re-affirm their loyalty. The foundation charter of Salisbury is dated 'at Hastings 1091' and three years later the king and his court were at the castle for a month. Whilst here, he attended the dedication of Battle Abbey, and received a stinging rebuke from Archbishop Anselm for failing to check the immorality of his young men, who 'grew their hair like girls and ... were in the habit of walking with their hair pranked and making irreligious gestures and walking mincingly'.[10]

Rufus also perpetrated a major fraud at Hastings, though from a distance. From France, he sent orders that the fyrd, the medieval conscript army, should assemble at Hastings and embark to join him. Each Hundred provided a certain number of men for the fyrd and furnished each of these with money to buy provisions while in the king's service. The fyrd, 20,000 strong, duly arrived at Hastings, only to have this subsistence money collected from them and to be told to return home. It meant easy money for Rufus but it was hard on the fyrd and even harder on Hastings, which took the brunt of the men's resentment.

The most notable of the many medieval royal visits was by John in 1201, for it was during this stay that he issued the famous ordinance on the Sovereignty of the Sea, which declared that any ships that did not 'strike or veil their bonnets' at the command of the King's Admiral or his lieutenant would be regarded as enemies. This ordinance is of great historical significance but it was to be the last time that Hastings was directly involved in anything so politically momentous. There were further royal visits and even further ordinances issued from the town, but none of these was noteworthy and the last of them, signed by Edward I in 1274, marked the end of the centre-stage importance that the town had enjoyed for so long.

It also marked the beginning of the end of its power as a Cinque Port. The last major engagement in which the part played by Hastings matched that of the other ports was the defeat of the French off St Mahe in 1293. After that, its decline was rapid. It was able to provide 30 ships for the king's service in 1335 but seven years later could equip only two, and, although it managed to send five ships to the Siege of Calais in 1347, it had been necessary to buy one of these from Winchelsea.

The decline was occasioned by what a witness in an enquiry of 1587 into the former land ownings of the castle collegiate church termed 'the frettinge and raginge of the sea'[11] and by the effects of the eastward drift; also by a number of destructive raids by the French. The result was the loss of what had been a renowned harbour.

Between 1292 and 1340 the Sussex coast lost a total of 5,500 acres of land to the sea, and Hastings suffered as badly as anywhere. A large section of the Castle Cliff fell *c.*1330 and a few years later there were further losses in the parishes of St Michael, St Peter and St Margaret. Elsewhere there was flooding. By the early 15th century the situation had become so bad that the Priory of the Holy Trinity, which had been founded some 250 years earlier and was sited just north of the present main Post Office, abandoned the unending struggle with the sea and moved to a new foundation at Warbleton, leaving only a token membership at Hastings.

Weakened and demoralised by the damage and losses, the town was unable to save itself from attack, let alone contribute effectively to the defence of the nation. The French capitalised on this and their raids were frequent and devastating. They were able to land in 1339 and to burn Hastings' boats and a large part of the town, and even to raid the castle. There was probably not a lot left there to steal because for some years there had been complaints about the walls being so ruinous that the townsfolk were busily despoiling it by day and by night.

Nevertheless, the affront stung Edward III's pride. Angered to hear 'that his foreign enemies, with ships and galleys, had lately landed at the port of Hastings, and his castle of the same had hostilely invaded and had thence carried away divers goods and as well had committed other depredations'[12], he ordered that improvements should be made in the castle's defences. It was to little avail. In 1377 the French landed again, and again robbed and burned the town.

The great days were definitely over. Town and castle continued to decay together, the former becoming no more than a large fishing village and the latter degenerating into a picturesque ruin as more and more of it fell into the sea. In 1588 Hastings was able to send only one reasonably sized ship, the 70-ton *Anne Bonaventure*, to join the fleet that put out against the Spanish Armada, and that was the very last time that it fulfilled any Cinque Port naval obligations.

Inevitably, the outside world and its affairs intruded from time to time but thereafter the town was no longer central to important issues. In the Civil War, Colonel Morley, the 'crooked rebel of Sussex', was here briefly, causing a couple of royalist clergymen to flee; in the Napoleonic era,

14 The battery was important to Hastings' defences until after the Napoleonic period and the Town Gunner, not to be confused with the man who afterwards fired the town's ceremonial guns on festive occasions, was a person of consequence.

15 The last of the local Martello towers, erected in anticipation of Napoleon's invasion, was demolished in the 1880s, after being undermined by the sea. The four towers at St Leonards, nos. 39-42, were built on the beach between Bo-Peep and Bulverhythe, 600 yards apart.

Martello towers and barracks were built in anticipation of invasion and Sir John Moore and Sir Arthur Wellesley, later Duke of Wellington, were stationed here. The town, though, remained a backwater, moving quietly, but with increasing self-importance, from fishing village to watering place and eventually to seaside resort.

The only time it came close to having a direct influence on history was when the confusion in its streets caused an accident in which the young Princess Victoria, then staying with her mother at 57, Marina, could easily have been killed. The horses pulling the royal carriage bolted and one of them fell. A workman brought the other to a halt. A gentleman, Peckham Micklethwaite, held the head of the fallen horse and then handed the future queen and her mother down from the carriage. The workman was thanked and the gentleman was created a baronet.

Such was the changed nature of the history of Hastings. It ceased to be the story of a town with a major part to play in the affairs of the nation but became more a matter of social history, more introverted, to do primarily with the people who lived in the town–the rich and the poor, the poets and the politicians, the artists and the soldiers, the famous and the infamous, the ordinary and the extraordinary–and the ways that they were affected by change and the ways that they changed the town in which they lived.

Chapter Two

Chopbacks and Fisherfolk

THE link between past and present Hastings is the fishing community. Apart from the castle and one or two churches, there are no truly ancient buildings in the town but the fishermen are part of an unbroken tradition that goes back probably to the original founding of Hastings and certainly to well before the Conquest.

The first Hastingers were fishermen when they were not being sea-raiders and their descendants were, until well into the 19th century, pirates and smugglers when they were not being fishermen. In the Middle Ages, Hastings was arguably the leading fishing port in the country. There were prolific fishing grounds nearby and the boats also went further afield after the herring that made up such an important part of the medieval diet.

Salted herrings were so valued that rents were often paid in them, and in 1329 a Hastings priest narrowly escaped excommunication for failing to provide the 2,000 herrings due annually to the Bishop of Chichester. As part of his penance, he agreed to 'pay to the bier of St Richard 20s sterling and to distribute 40s sterling among the poor parishioners of the church of Bulwarhithe'.[1]

Fishermen from Hastings and the other Cinque Ports made Yarmouth their headquarters during the herring season and their annual visit clearly dated from before the town was properly established, since they long retained control of the great Herring Fair held there at Michaelmas. Merchants from as far afield as France and Flanders attended the fair, which was administered and policed by the bailiffs of the Cinque Ports.

16 Even after the Cinque Ports lost control of Yarmouth, the herring fishery remained all-important. However, immediately prior to the First World War, things became so bad that many fishermen emigrated to Canada. It was only the export of herrings to Russia that kept the local fishing fleet in business.

Naturally this supervision, which did not finally end until 1663, was bitterly resented and led to the most serious inter-town feud of the Middle Ages. This culminated in a full-scale battle between the East Anglian and Cinque Ports' fleets in 1297 off the coast of Flanders, after Edward I and his army had been landed at Sluys. The Cinque Ports triumphed, killing 165 of the East Anglians, burning 17 of their ships and looting another 12 ships.

17 There was a big local trade in smoked herrings–one trader claimed to have sold 2,000 in one Saturday afternoon and evening in George Street. A long smoking produced 'red herrings', a shorter one, bloaters, if they were smoked whole, and kippers if they were first split and gutted.

It is a reminder that the fishermen were also the fighting force of the Cinque Ports. Their services were so invaluable that as well as the written charters granted them there was also a tacit acceptance of the lawlessness and violence for which they, and the Hastings men particularly, were noted. Piracy was very much part of their tradition and no stray ship encountered in the Channel was safe from them. Yarmouth ships were always fair game and a number of such attacks had helped to fuel the resentment that erupted at Sluys.

The taste for piracy lingered and it has frequently been said that Hastings fishermen acquired their nickname of Chopbacks in the 18th century after those responsible for an attack on a Dutch merchantman were identified when they boasted of how the Dutch captain had wriggled when chopped down the back by the axe. However, the true origin of the name is probably older than that. The axe was the traditional weapon of the early Hastingers–in the Middle Ages a raised axe was the greetings salute for a Hastings boat–and the smash to the spine was a favoured blow.

With France and England so often at war, there were long periods when piracy became almost a patriotic duty and was actively encouraged by the king, who took a share of the profits. Henry II actually ordered the Cinque Ports to attack the French at every opportunity. They obeyed him enthusiastically, the French retaliated and so for many years there was a reign of terror in the Channel and along the Channel coasts.

It was always profit, though, that motivated the Cinque Ports men and their loyalty had to be bought. In 1203 they threatened to withdraw from England and to exist as rootless pirates. In 1216 they actually joined forces with the French for a while, returning to their allegiance only after the king had produced a big enough bribe. They then defeated their erstwhile allies in a battle off Sandwich.

18 Until the fishermen started using their own motor winches in the late 1930s, the larger boats were pulled up the beach by council-owned horse capstans. The annual Stade dues paid for the maintenance of these and there was also a winding fee payable each time one was used. The horses were stabled in Rock-a-Nore Road.

19 Smaller boats did not need the council's horse capstans but were winched up by their own smaller capstans operated by human muscle-power. This picture, though, is obviously posed.

They were also quite prepared to go to war on their own behalf. This happened in 1293, when, angered by the killing of some Portsmen by the Normans, they took a bloody, but also profitable, revenge. A contemporary account said that 'they slew with the sword their enemies who came to encounter them, and threw their carcasses into the sea, without respect to their rank, and did not let one single survivor escape, and brought back their vessels and baggage and wines, and other necessaries to their own homes, and all the contents of their ships, dividing the ships and their spoils among themselves'.[2]

After this, Hastings went into the decline detailed in Chapter 1, but this did not mean that the old fighting spirit was entirely lost. The wars of the 18th and early 19th centuries provided new opportunities for legalised piracy, with privateers being licensed to prey on enemy shipping. The opportunity was eagerly accepted by Hastingers and many privateers were commissioned locally.

One was the *Greyhound*, commanded by Captain Solomon Bevill, which had a noteworthy encounter with a French privateer off Beachy Head in December 1778. Although heavily out-manned and out-gunned–the Frenchman had a crew of 120 and mounted 14 six-pounder guns against the *Greyhound*'s 25 men and 10 four-pounders–Captain Bevill engaged with the enemy, which, after a prolonged running fight, yielded to him. By then the Frenchman had seven dead and 21 wounded, two of them fatally. The French guns having fired too high, the *Greyhound* had just two men wounded.

Much the same spirit was demonstrated in 1798, when a French privateer sailed audaciously close to Hastings and took a boat carrying lime, then an important item of trade. Some of the fishermen hastily collected a few firearms and launched their boats in pursuit and 'the whole town, including the visitors, became spectators of the chase'.[3] This was successful. The lime boat was recovered and 'before the sun set, the French sailors were deposited in the cage or prison in the High Street'.

Such incidents could have come straight from the Hornblower genre of sea stories but not all the engagements were so gallant. Some local crews could not resist the easy pickings offered by neutral merchantmen, and in 1759 the commanders of two Hastings privateers and four members of their crew were executed after such an attack. Their haul had been 20 casks of butter. Then there were the tactics of fishing boats armed with a carronade apiece that went in search of quicker returns than fishing could provide. Their crews had no intention of taking part in ship-to-ship gun battles. They were after profits not glory, and their preferred manoeuvre was to get alongside on pretence of trade, take the other crew by surprise and confine them below, then ransack the ship before sinking it.

This ruthless pragmatism demonstrated clearly that the Jutish blood of their ancestors had not been overly thinned by the centuries. Nor is this surprising for then, and perhaps for another hundred years or so, the men and women of the fishing community were still very largely the lineal descendants of the original Hastingers, distinct in appearance, speech and attitude from all around them. As a writer of 1833 put it, 'There is about the Hastings Fisherman a characteristic stamp, which is not to be met with in any other class of man in the island.'[4]

Part of that 'characteristic stamp' but discreetly ignored then and frequently glossed over since, was the tendency to lawlessness and violence and a reluctance to accept any sort of imposed authority. Through the centuries they were always willing to exchange their fishing boats for war galleys, pirate ships or privateers, and smuggling craft. It was in their blood. Smuggling, whether of men or goods, was a profitable sideline for at least 600 years, from the 13th century on into the 19th.

Hastings was mentioned specifically when a commission was set up in 1274 to enquire into the illegal export of wool, and it

20 As well as the distinct physical stamp remarked on by early writers, Old Towners long retained a dialect showing marked differences to that spoken elsewhere in Sussex. Words such as 'frap' (to hit) and 'boco' (plenty of) betrayed a strong French influence.

was local boatmen who obliged when a man condemned to death at the castle needed to be smuggled across the Channel to safety. Castle canons had rescued the man 'by force of arms' and given him sanctuary for eight days before arranging for him 'to cross over the Straits in a small boat'.[5] Nearly 400 years later an abortive scheme to effect the escape of Charles I, then at Carisbrooke Castle, involved having 'a bark at Hastings in readiness to carry him into France'.[6]

Until the mid-17th century, smuggling was almost entirely the export smuggling of wool, sometimes termed owling. This was big business. It was claimed in the 17th century that the majority of the fleeces of the 160,000 sheep on Romney Marsh would be 'sent off hot into France'.[7] Many went out from Hastings and Hastings men were among the gangs that 'rode, armed with guns, bludgeons and clubs, throughout the country, setting everyone at defiance, and awing all the quiet inhabitants'.[8] As with the later and more publicised 'brandy for the parson' type of smuggling, there was a great deal of muddled thinking about the morality of this and one Hastings man, George Lopdale, considered himself unjustly imprisoned for his involvement. He complained that the wool had not been his but his brother's and all that he had done had been to carry it to the seashore.

Import smuggling began to add to the profits of this wool trade in 1638 when a ban on the import of caps and hats immediately made it worthwhile to smuggle these into the country. Hastingers behaved predictably. In 1640, the official appointed to search out the smugglers in the town reported aggrievedly that although he had found 'five dozen and three' hats in 'the howse of one John Spy of Hasteings' his attempts to recover them had failed, largely because 'the officer of whom your petitioner required ayd (being the said Spies neighbour and freind) refused to assist him'.[9]

21 The Wishing Tree was formerly known as the Smugglers' Oak because it was where an ambush was set for a gang of smugglers transporting goods inland. One smuggler was killed but the others escaped. The name Wishing Tree was supposedly first used in a story that a man (Robert Deudney) made up and told his child.

However, the real mushroom growth of smuggling came when the 18th-century wars with France made it hugely profitable to bring in spirits and other luxury goods. In a lecture delivered at the Music Hall in 1871 and later published in book form,[10] John Banks, by then the highly respected headmaster of the Grammar School but whose family had been closely involved in smuggling, declared that a tub of spirits bought for perhaps 10s. 6d. in France 'would sell easily for 3 or even 4 pounds or guineas'. He added that smugglers reckoned to make a profit even if they lost two cargoes out of three, and the scale of the trade is demonstrated by the details he gave of one seizure at Hastings in 1805. This included 477 casks of brandy, amounting to 1,650 gallons, and 421 casks of gin (1,460 gallons) as well as quantities of rum, tea and tobacco. It had a total value of £2,784 5s. 8d. That was a lot of money in 1805, and far more cargoes got through than were seized.

The whole town was involved in the trade. In a court case some years later, Charles Picknell, Pier Warden at Hastings, declared, 'You were not thought respectable then if you were not a smuggler'. Asked if this applied to the whole town, he replied, 'Oh yes; they were all smugglers–parsons and all'. Sweeping though it was, this statement received support from Banks, who stressed that it was not 'the lower classes only who were engaged in this traffic, but the middle and upper classes also' and told of 'a lady of exalted station' who, on hearing that a run had been intercepted, expressed the hope that 'it was not the parson's boat'.

John Campbell, who in 1836 became Inspector of the newly created Hastings Police Force, admitted in his reminiscences[11] that it had been the profit on a smuggling venture that had enabled him to get married. He had towed ashore a line of roped tubs from a lugger off the Pier Rocks and then, on receiving a signal that the coast was clear, he and each of the other waiting men, 'took up his load and walked away with it up the Parade steps ... to certain hiding places'. For that, he received 10s. and a half anker of brandy, which he sold for £3 8s. So his exploit had, as he put it, 'furnished me with a nice little sum wherewith to accomplish my projected marriage'.

Hiding places abounded in the Old Town. Banks said that in his family home in Russell Court there were three hidey holes: a large unused oven in the kitchen; a closet in one of the bedrooms; and 'a large excavation which had been made specially for the purpose of concealing casks of spirits' under the pig-sty in the backyard. Other houses were even better equipped. According to another writer who claimed first-hand knowledge, 'in one case the Smuggler's hole is under the floor of a living room, in several others roomy recesses built in the walls each side of the fireplace and the openings hidden from view by the cosy seats, and in several others an entire double floor, with sufficient space between to take 40-50 tubs; the floor is loosened by a secret spring'.[12]

Almost every house in Old Town was a safe house and the smugglers did not hesitate to take refuge or store goods anywhere if the need arose. Banks recalled his father on one occasion being very annoyed at having 100 casks dumped on him, the more so as one of them had been damaged and he was afraid that the smell of the spirits would carry to the nearby home of an exciseman.

The major storage places, though, especially when a run inland was being planned, were various large hidey holes and barns in lonely parts of the town and surrounding countryside. Beggars' Hole on the way to Crowhurst was one such. There was also Buckshole and another Smugglers' Hole in the nearby Newgate Wood. The barns used included one at Warrior Square, which was a favoured landing place, being lonely and possessing tracks running off to Bohemia and Gensing. This barn was known as the Warehouse, pronounced Warrus; hence, according to one school of thought, the eventual gentrification into Warrior Square.

For night landings, lights were used to let the boats know which landing place was safe. A flint and steel produced a spark easily seen out at sea on a dark night, but unlikely to be spotted by anyone else. One signalling place was on the cliff at Bo-Peep, which is said to have inspired the 'Little Bo-Peep' rhyme, the sheep being ships and their tails the strings of tubs that they towed behind

22 The building on the left housed the Lower Light. The Hastings fishermen were guided ashore by the Upper and Lower Lights; they were in a safe channel when the lights were in line. The Lower Light was rebuilt in 1827 and the Upper was moved from the George Street Light Steps to the West Hill in 1851.

them. These tails were often sunk off the mouth of the Asten and later hauled up into the timbered outlet of the river.

Not all landings were made at night. One strategem used for a while was to disguise the tubs with plaster of Paris and bring them in quite openly as if part of one of the cargoes of chalk frequently landed at Hastings. On one occasion, a gang was caught red-handed whilst brazenly unloading tubs. There was such an open-and-shut case against them that it seemed a waste of money when the leader, Philip Kent, hired Lawyer Langham, known as the Smugglers' Lawyer, for the defence. Langham insisted that before sentence was pronounced, a tub should be brought in to court and sampled to prove the allegation. The sampling provoked a great spluttering among the magistrates for the tub, like each of the others that had been impounded, was filled with salt water.

It had been a set-up. The real cargo, safely roped and buoyed some way out, had been picked up by another boat and landed elsewhere whilst Kent and his crew made a great show of unloading their tubs of salt-water. Kent went on to become a well-known boat-builder and owner of several of the hoys bringing coal to the town and died, much respected, in 1873, aged 88.

Such stories create an admiration for the smugglers, and Banks endowed them with an almost Arcadian innocence when he described how it was customary 'for people connected with the contraband trade to assemble in small parties of 10 or 12 on the East and West Hills on a summer's evening for the purpose of regaling themselves with brandy and milk and enjoying a pipe therewith'. He also insisted that the Hastings smugglers never went armed and 'once fairly caught, they generally gave in'.

This simply was not the case. There were countless individual acts of violence and many pitched battles, a number of which resulted in loss of life. The smugglers killed a customs man at Bulverhythe in 1734 and between then and 1833, when a company of the Rifle Brigade had to make a forced march from Dover to Hastings after an affray in which a coastguard had been killed, there were numerous deaths and injuries on both sides.

In the 1830s, improvements to the Customs Service combined with a lowering of import duties brought the great days of smuggling to an end, and came close to being the ruin of many Hastings fishermen. They had become used to easy money but were suddenly reduced to reliance on their legitimate trade, and at a time when this was becoming less profitable.

Previously, fishing had been the mainstay of the town, so much so that, in the mid-17th century, of the 280 heads of household, 239 were directly involved with fishing or some other activity connected with the sea. Consequently, the statement, often repeated, that when the town lost its importance as a Cinque Port it rapidly sank to extreme poverty, is a little misleading. It refers to the Corporation rather than to individuals, who prospered or did not prosper in much the same degree as the inhabitants of any other town. Hastings was no longer able to supply the sort of ships needed for naval service and could not afford to build a harbour, but its shipyards retained a high reputation and it continued to be a major supplier of fish to the London market throughout the later Middle Ages and the 17th and 18th centuries.

The records of the fisheries of those times have a curiously modern ring. There was much concern regarding over-fishing and about unfair competition from the French and the restrictions to which Hastings fishermen were subjected. The size of nets was strictly regulated and heavy fines were imposed for fishing out of season. In 1561 there was a Cinque Ports' decree that if 'any hath taken yong Fry of Fish with any Nettes that be straight and too narrow Mokes whereby the increase of any fish is destroyed or minished, his paine is to make a greivous Fine at ye will of the Lord Admirall'.[13]

The season for plaice and sole and 'such like fish' was between 'ye 15th day of March' and 'ye feast of All Saints' and anyone fishing

23 Henry I's own ship was built at Hastings over 800 years ago and sizeable boats continued to be built here until the early 1950s. In the 19th century, the major yards were those of Thwaites and Winter, shown here, and Ransom and Ridley. There are stories of local witches interfering with the launches from these yards.

24 Mending the nets was a never-ending task. Moss commented in 1824 on the damage done to the nets by dogfish attacking the herring caught in them, and claimed that 'the destructive fish' could make 3,000 holes in a net in one night. This supposedly explains the local name of robin huss (robbing us) for this fish.

outside these limits was fined 40s. The same amount was levied on anyone convicted of having 'drawne for plaise and Soles' between sunset and sunrise, for it was considered essential to 'suffer such fish quietly without any disturbance to have his Nightly feeding and nourishing'. In 1604, the mounting concern of the other Cinque Ports that the trawls used by Hastings boats were 'great destroyers of the fry and food of fish' resulted in them being banned and the Lord Warden empowered his agents to cut in pieces or burn any that they found still in use.

Then, as now, the French were accused of fishing out of season, of using illegal nets and invading the local fishing grounds. There were repeated complaints that so many of the French were exploiting local waters that Hastings fishermen found it hard to make a living. Feelings ran high and often spilled over into violence, with the Hastings boats attempting to drive the French away. At least once, in 1616, there was an exchange of shots.

The end of the smuggling boom in the 1830s coincided with the Hastings fishermen encountering increased competition from bigger boats, many of them French, that were able to undercut them in the vital London market. Nor was this the only problem that they had to face. The end of smuggling had also marked a sea change in the nature of Hastings itself. It embraced respectability. The seaside had become fashionable and a new Hastings developed to cater for that fashion. The town expanded westward to fill the Priory valley and then to stretch further along the coast to join with the elegant, custom-built resort of St Leonards. Many of the developers and the tradesmen and workers who flocked to the town to take advantage of the opportunities that it offered felt no kinship with old Hastings.

After nearly 2,000 years, the fishing quarter was no longer the heart of the town and the fishermen found themselves increasingly sidelined and even regarded as obstacles to progress. They did not fit the new image of Hastings. True, they and their cottages and the paraphernalia of their trade had a certain picturesque value, being fit subjects for artists and, later in the century, photographers, and a great many rather patronising words were written about them, but in real life they were seen as uncomfortable neighbours, too wont to show an uninhibited enjoyment of life and to demonstrate an obstinate independence. Also, they occupied, rather messily, an area of the beach and Sea Front that cried out for sanitised improvement.

25 Making shell ornaments and decorating everything from boxes to needlebooks with shells to tempt visitors to buy became a cottage industry with the fishermen's wives and daughters.

26 & 27 Both of these views show the encroachment on what had always been a working beach, and the diminishing number of net shops and boats. The coasting brig shown in the first picture is anchored near the Pier Rocks, the probable site of the Elizabethan harbour destroyed by storms, rebuilt and destroyed again in 1596.

28 While nobody can be sure of the origins of the unique net shops, their design possibly results from the need years ago for storage space for three separate sets of nets and equipment–for mackerel fishing, herring fishing and trawling–plus a charge made calculated on the area of ground occupied.

29 The line of washing strung up between the boats remained a common sight up to the beginning of the Second World War, as few homes in the crowded Old Town had back gardens. Earlier, when many women in Old Town took in washing from the hotels and lodging houses, the beach was often festooned with laundry.

30 The Round Fishmarket, or Rotunda, where fish was sold to the general public, was built opposite the bottom of High Street in 1870 and demolished in 1928. It occupied part of what is now the car park.

31 The fishmarket in 1937. A wholesale fishmarket was built opposite East Beach Street in 1901-2. Previously the selling had been much as described by Moss in 1824, with the fish shot out on the beach and sold by Dutch auction, 'when the seller begins with his own price and falls, until some one cries out–"I will have it".' No licence fee had to be paid when running a Dutch auction.

32 The out-door fishmarket in 1910. In 1833, the council tried to close the open-air market and force all fish sellers to use a new market built in George Street. Those who refused to leave their traditional pitches were jailed. The fishermen then stormed the jail en masse to secure their release. They were also promised that the Stade market could continue.

33 The ship-keeper of the *Enterprise*, at work in his net shop. The *Enterprise*, now preserved in the Fishermen's Museum, was one of the last of the big sailing ships without engines to be built in Hastings. She was built in 1912 at a cost of £700 and was presented to the Museum in 1955, having become too old to continue fishing.

The Corporation started to talk about road widening schemes as early as 1824 and in 1833 made an attempt to clear the fishmarket from its traditional site that failed only because it stirred up the old Hastinger spirit and provoked a riot that frightened officialdom into retreat. Selling fish from the beach was banned and those who defied this edict were imprisoned, but about one hundred fishermen stormed the jail and had already broken down the part of the outer wall when the Mayor lost his nerve and ordered the prisoners' release.

Since then, it is probably true to say that the fishing community has felt continuously under threat as much from the Council as from changing conditions in the fishing industry. Somehow, though, both the Old Town community and the fishing fleet have survived, and long may they continue to do so. It would be sad indeed should there come a time when there were no true Hastingers living and working in Old Town and the only remaining boats and net houses were ones carefully preserved as museum exhibits, part of a Hastings Old Town Experience.

Chapter Three

Politics and Other Diversions

THE claim that England's first tournament was held in Hastings Castle, with William's daughter Adela as Queen of Beauty, is almost certainly unjustified. It is possible, though, that the town could claim another entertainment first–the possession of the country's first municipal orchestra, and that over 800 years ago. Admittedly it would be a tongue-in-cheek claim but it is true that in 1260 Henry III ordered the bailiff and barons of the town 'to cause ten or twelve good men of Hastings to come to Westminster and to send a boat ornamented with banners and supplied with young men and trumpets who may play on the water of Thames under Westminster for the recreation of the king and others'.[1]

However, evidence though this may be of an early musical tradition, it has to be admitted that the general preference of Hastingers was always for more robust, even rumbustious, pleasures. They compensated for the harshness of their daily lives with such seasonal enjoyments as the May-day revelries and guising (pronounced geezing), when everyone paraded in disguises and masks, which was eventually banned by Henry VIII as a heathenish practice. The guising season was from Hallowe'en to Candlemas, which suggests a reason for Guy Fawkes celebrations later being embraced so enthusiastically in Hastings and East Sussex.

They also showed a zestful enjoyment of market days and fairs and an uninhibited acceptance of the opportunities for feasting and drinking and making a joyful noise

34 The Hastings and St Leonards Bonfire Boys about to embark on a robust celebration of 5 November 1910.

35 When Victoria was crowned, in 1838 local celebrations included a mock coronation in All Saints parish, with Ann Page installed as Queen. She was 'a sprightly old dame of 69 or 70' renowned for her attendance at all dances and merrymakings. She could be considered the town's first Carnival Queen.

36 The Floral Fête, 1895. Hastings' first carnival was based very much on the famous event at Nice, hence the Floral Fête and the Battle of Confetti. But locals resented the enclosure of the Parade and roadway at Eversfield Place and broke through to watch without paying.

37 The carnival originated in 1895. It was revived after the Second World War but lost impetus and, after the Old Town started organising its own procession in 1968, it lost support and was soon given up. Meanwhile the Old Town carnival, seen here in 1974, is the centre-piece of Old Town Week and continues to attract large crowds.

provided by occasional local and national rejoicings, and by politics. For centuries, this meant the assemblies at the Hundred Place, near the town wall and on the site of what became Winding Lane, at which the bailiff and his fellow barons conducted the town's business and were themselves appointed.

Any resident of substance and any newcomer 'using some honest craft and being of good conversation for a year and a day'[2] could be granted the franchise and so become a freeman, or baron of the Cinque Ports. The barons elected 12 jurats as the bailiff's 'brethren', and these swore to help him in his duties and the administration of justice. It was from the ranks of the jurats that the freemen annually chose the bailiff, who after 1588 became known as the mayor. All these elections cost the men who were elected. Each freeman and jurat paid a fine which went into the town chest but each, and this included the bailiff, was also expected to show a wider liberality and pay for the slaking of the general thirst.

In 1356, a man and his son 'satisfied the bailiff and commonalty with one cask of wine'[3] but when the great Whig politician, the Duke of Newcastle, then still Lord Clare, was made a freeman in 1714, it cost him £388 18s. 7d. and there were heavy scores to settle at the town's inns.

Newcastle also spent freely on parliamentary elections at Hastings, which was a pocket borough managed by his agent, John Collier. Since the Tory candidates also tried to buy success, elections in the 18th century became as good as fair days and were much enjoyed in a town where very few had

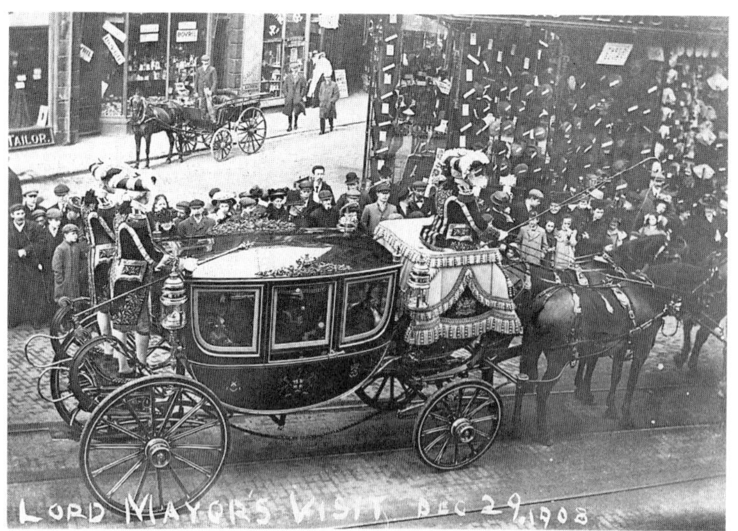

38 Lord Mayor's visit, 1908. This procession was apparently just a treat for the town provided by the Lord Mayor because he had a weekend home in St Leonards. He brought the coach down by rail. Another Lord Mayor, Alderman Stone, built Castleham Mansion at Hollington and the Hastings banker, Thomas Farncomb, became Lord Mayor in 1849.

39 Crowds turned out in 1891 to catch a glimpse of Gladstone, the Grand Old Man of British politics. The Gaiety Theatre was filled to capacity for his speech of 1½ hours long. He is pictured here leaving Hastings railway station after lunching in the second-class restaurant.

40 The first Christ Church was built in London Road in 1860 by Lady St John and her son, Rev. Charles Lyndhurst Vaughan, who became its first priest. He established the tradition of Anglo-Catholic worship and was one of the many notable church leaders that the town has known.

a vote but all had thirsts and were happy to satisfy them with both Whig and Tory beer. In those days, Hastings had two M.P.s and until the 1832 Reform Bill these were returned by the votes of just 12 jurats and 18 freemen, but the whole town enjoyed the campaigns and even, to some extent, the violence that was part and parcel of the process.

Nor did things change very much immediately after the Reform Bill. Until the introduction of the secret ballot in 1872, candidates had to declare themselves and were voted for at the public hustings, which gave all and sundry the chance to make their feelings known. If anything, violence worsened after the Reform Bill, perhaps because the widening of the franchise increased the frustrations of those who were still without a vote. The local historian T.B. Brett thought that the election of 1852 was the most riotous of any that he had witnessed.

It was bad enough on Nomination Day, when 4,000 crowded into hustings at Priory Meadow and made so much noise that the speakers could not make themselves heard, but it was even worse the next day, when the results were declared. The winning candidates were Patrick Robertson and Wastrel Brisco, but the mayor refused to announce this until the 'bludgeon men' in Mr. Robertson's procession had been

41 & 42 Two photographs of the Albert Memorial and York Buildings. The picture above was taken in 1863, only a year after the memorial had been erected in memory of the Prince Consort, and is a reminder that the original development in what is now the town centre was largely residential. The picture to the left was taken around the turn of the 19th century.

43 A 1907 motor parade was another of the special events organised to brighten and widen the appeal of Hastings.

44 Tremendous interest was aroused in 1909 when, to demonstrate the value of motor transport, members of the A.A. used their own cars to bring a battalion of Guards from London to Hastings. In 1955 the event was re-enacted, using appropriate vintage cars. Mr. F.S. Bennett, shown here, led both the 1909 run and that of 1955.

45 & 46 Fairlight Cottage decorated for Edward VII's Coronation in 1902 and Woolworth's decorated for Elizabeth II's Coronation in 1953. On both occasions, a great many celebratory events were organised in the town and the mayors and others were accorded their traditional right as Barons of the Cinque Ports to attend the ceremonies.

disarmed and their weapons confiscated. When he did give out the result, it proved very unpopular. The crowd would not let the new M.P.s address their supporters and, when they left in their victory procession, pelted them with turves torn up from the meadow.

The uproar continued as the long procession–it was said that as the head of it emerged from All Saints Street the final carriage was only just entering High Street–toured the town. Robertson's agent was pulled from his horse, fisherwomen jostled and punched the men carrying the banners and a series of running fights had to be broken up by the police. There was a constant chorus of cat-calls and abuse, especially in Old Town, and a newspaper reported that 'Dust and flour flew in clouds, while even grosser substances were made use of', and considered it 'marvellous the excited horses did not trample some of the crowd under foot'.[4]

Such political excitement was not seen again locally until the era of the suffragettes. The 'Votes for Women' campaign got under way early in Hastings and by the early 1880s the local branch of the London National Society for Women's Suffrage was holding regular drawing-room meetings and attracting audiences of up to one hundred. The society was active from the very beginning. By 1884 its secretary, Miss Fricker Hall, was exchanging letters with Gladstone and pamphlets were published that went on sale in local bookshops. One, *Reasons for the Enfranchisement of Women*, was written by Madame Bodichon, née Barbara Leigh Smith, who started the feminist magazine, *The Englishwoman's Journal*, and co-founded what became Girton College. She came in regularly from her home at Robertsbridge to help and encourage the Hastings ladies. Another 'name' was Olive Schreiner, author of *The Story of an African Farm*, who became a member of the society when she was living in St Leonards in 1884.

The general level of the membership was very high, for Hastings housed a quite

TO THE

ELECTORS

OF

Hastings and St. Leonards.

MY name is HOWARD ELPHINSTONE,
I'm neither Whig nor Tory;
A RADICAL REFORMER I,
Free trade is all my glory.

On foreign Grain I will maintain
The Tax a Spoliation;
Of People, Farmers, Landlords too
The downright ruination.

Taxes on all should lightly fall,
But lightest on the classes,
That now called lower, are burdened more
And treated worse than asses.

Lawgivers born I hold in scorn
And rooted detestation;
Coblers and Tinkers are deeper thinkers,
And best at legislation.

The Baronet's cheer should be small beer,
While you get drunk with brandy;
Your wives regale with toast and ale,
Your brats suck sugar-candy.

Tho' Warre may sing of Church and King
And North of Constitution;
Down with them all---they soon must fall
If you've but resolution.

Connection between Church and State
My mind's too pure to think on;
The only course is a divorce
In such a case of Crim. Con.

To give no handle to farther scandal
The parties I would sever;
Old Mother Church, left in the lurch,
Should lose her Tithes for ever.

On bread and water I'd Bishops quarter,
And free them from temptation
To think of aught with fervent thought
Save Heavenly Translation.

If I'd my swing, I down would bring
Both Palace, Church and Steeple;
No WILL I'd own save that alone
Of you, most Sovereign People.

The Bill's my guide, and nought beside,
I'll stick unto its letter;
And add the Ballot, to suit your palate,
And make it work the better.

So if with me you all agree,
And think my notions clever;
Give me your votes, and rend your throats
With ELPHINSTONE for ever.

*** *The above may be Sung to the Tune of Mrs. Caisey.*

ORE PLACE, *September 12th*, 1832.

47 Despite this manifesto, which won him great popularity in the town, Elphinstone did not get elected until 1835. Amongst the noteworthy men who have represented Hastings were Edmund Waller, the poet, in the Cavalier Parliament of 1661 and the famous George Canning, who whilst M.P. for Hastings fought a duel with Castlereagh in 1809.

disproportionate number of well-educated women of independent means and with close links with the world of the arts, literature and the stage, where the concepts of female rights and the 'new woman' were widely discussed and supported. It was significant that the writer Sarah Grand, credited with coining the term 'new woman', attended the inaugural meeting of the Hastings Suffrage Society, one of the several societies, large and small, that were eventually represented in the town. Add to all this the local leadership of some very strong and remarkable women (see chapter 7) and it is not surprising that the Hastings feminists were so active and, eventually, so militant.

As well as a regular programme of 'At Homes', public meetings, open-air speeches, rallies, poster parades and processions, they organised self-denial weeks and lantern slide entertainments and even sold ice-cream from a suffragette barrow. They also interrupted theatre programmes and church services, sabotaged several pillar boxes and were accused, possibly unfairly, of planting an incendiary device in Holy Trinity Church and of burning down Levetleigh, one-time home of the borough M.P.

Naturally, this made them fair game for the hooligan element, which itself enjoyed breaking up their meetings and giving various of them some pretty rough handling. In 1914, soon after the fire at Levetleigh, this escalated into full-scale mob violence. The first riot developed in St Leonards in March, on a day, afterwards referred to locally as Black Wednesday, when goods seized from the home of Mrs. Darent Harrison were due to be auctioned to meet a tax bill. As part of her suffrage campaign, Mrs. Harrison was a leading light of the Tax Resistance League and on the principle of 'No Vote, No Tax' refused to pay the Inhabited House Duty.

On the day of the auction, she and her supporters organised a procession around the town to end at the auction rooms in Norman Road. It met with noisy opposition even before it set off from her home at 1 St Paul's Place and this opposition soon became violent. Fighting broke out and, even before they reached the Memorial, many of the women were extremely dishevelled and most of their banners had been torn from them or were ripped.

Back in St Leonards, the situation worsened and, when the procession reached Norman Road, the hostile crowd lost all restraint. The protecting police were pushed aside; one carriage was overturned and determined attacks were made on others, while the ladies in them defended themselves gamely with their umbrellas. Ladies on foot suffered attempts to tear off their clothing and, while some fought back courageously, others fled screaming for shelter. Some found refuge in a stable and others were besieged in a forge until the police regained control of the situation and were able to escort them clear of the battleground. Even then, it was some time before the crowd could be persuaded to disperse.

Two months later, on 20 May, there were similar scenes in Hastings, when the Suffrage Club in Havelock Road was attacked by a mob that grew from 300 at 8.40 p.m. to an estimated 3,000 by 9 p.m. Flour, eggs and stones were thrown at the building and, when the frightened ladies sought to escape, they were assailed by a cacophony of verbal abuse and even physical assault.

Miss Marchant, a Suffrage Society committee member and local schoolmistress, was struck violently in the back and head and had her hat, which had been secured with a large silver pin, torn from her head. A policeman managed to get her through to the bottom of Havelock Road and then urged her to run as fast as she could to the police station to take shelter.

Further up the road, there was fighting at the archway leading into Priory Street as the police struggled to hold back the mob and allow a number of women to make their escape that way. There were scuffles everywhere up and down the road and a constant din of shouting and screaming as the women ran the gauntlet of their attackers, receiving bruises and scratches and in some cases having their clothing torn from them. A witness later told of seeing one with her blouse 'pulled away to the extent that it showed her corset'. Another, screaming hysterically, escaped further rough handling

48 For many years the town's ceremonial guns were fired to mark all special occasions and celebrations.

49 The changeover from Royal Flying Corps to Royal Air Force brought George V to Hastings in 1918 to inspect a parade at South Saxons. Among those inspected was Prince Albert, later George VI, who was stationed here. These VADs and scouts also turned out in parade order in Filsham Road.

when her purse spilled open and her assailants scrabbled for the scattered coins.

Some women were able to get away quickly in cars before the crowd completely filled the road but headlights and car windows were smashed. The occupants of one car– Mrs. Strickland, Mrs. Raymond Pelly (grandchild of Elizabeth Fry), and Miss Pelly– had a particularly frightening experience. Before they got away, a man opened the door, grabbed hold of Miss Pelly and tried to drag her out of the car. No sooner had the two older ladies pulled her free than the other door was wrenched open and another man attempted to get in and had to be pulled back by a policeman. At that point, the chauffeur, hearing shouts of 'Turn it over!' ignored Mrs. Pelly's instruction to 'Drive slowly' and went off as fast as he could.

Three suffragists, the crowd at their heels, rushed into *Green's Hotel*, at the corner of Havelock Road and Priory Street, for refuge. Mr. Wade, the licensee, frightened that the stones that immediately smashed the windows presaged the total wrecking of his hotel, at first ordered the women out but eventually let them stay after they had signed an agreement to reimburse him for any damage that might be done.

The aftermath of all this was, if anything, even more discreditable than the mob violence because, when these three ladies later sued the corporation, under the Riot Damage Act, for the return of the money that they paid Mr. Wade, he and the mayor and the police united to deny that there had been any riot.

The mayor, Alderman Hutchings, said that he had been in Havelock Road that evening, had seen no-one molested and thought the crowd good-humoured and not particularly noisy. Superintendent Kenward had also been unaware of any atmosphere of threat and had witnessed far worse scenes at elections and on 5 November. Inspector Green went so far as to say that he had never known a much quieter crowd at Hastings, while Mr. Wade deposed that the crowd had been in holiday mood, was well controlled by the police and most people were there only out of curiosity.

The response of the judge was caustic and he was critical of the police for not having dispersed the crowd earlier and for not having made any arrests. He found that the ladies had suffered from the actions of a riotous mob and so were entitled to compensation. His verdict was greeted with cheers and shouts of 'Votes for Women'.

These anti-suffrage riots were provoked to some degree by the feeling that women were upsetting the natural order, turning the world on its head. Some years earlier there was the same sort of uneasiness and fear of change felt by many in Hastings but concerning religion rather than politics and the result was frequent public turmoil. Both High and Low Church practices came under attack. In February 1851, an effigy of the Pope was paraded about the town before being burned on the beach, and in the 1860s the high Anglican services at the newly built Christ Church in London Road aroused mob protest with the church attacked and services interrupted.

The worst of the disturbances, though, came when the Salvation Army started its activities locally. These were so disliked that in 1884 the council even took unsuccessful High Court action to try to stop the 'disturbance caused by the outdoor demonstrations and processions of this organisation'.[5]

Salvationist baiting became the great outdoor sport of gangs of youths, who, following the example set in other Sussex resorts, formed themselves into a rival Skeleton Army and aped the religious movement, holding their own processions and meetings and doing everything they could to ridicule and disrupt the other's activities. They were always threatening and the threats often spilled over into violence.

At the end of September 1884 there was a full-scale attack on the 'Iron Fort' in St Andrew's Square, where the Skeleton Army smashed windows and marched around the Square yelling and hooting. Police

50 As in every other town in the country, VE Day was celebrated with hastily organised street parties in every part of the borough. Fifty years on, many repeat parties were organised.

51 For the town's establishment, the Mayoral Ball was the event of the year.

intervention led to hand-to-hand fighting and the near-riot continued until nearly ten o'clock, when the Skeleton Army sang 'God Save the Queen' and 'Rule Britannia' and marched off to the Memorial and York Buildings, where there was more speech-making and stone throwing. It seems that the violence remains the same; only the excuse for it changes through the generations.

Fortunately, there were great gatherings in Hastings that did not generate ill will. Indeed, politics was responsible for the greatest single act of public celebration ever held in the town–the Reform Bill banquet of 1832. This took place in Priory Brooks, which covered the ground from Bank buildings and Havelock Rock through to St Andrew's Square and beyond; this space was needed because on 19 July 1832 some six thousand people, approximately sixty per cent of the town's total population, sat down to a feast of beef, mutton and potatoes and hot plum pudding washed down with huge quantities of beer.

The feasting over, thousands more from the town and the surrounding countryside arrived to enjoy the 'juggling matches, treacle-roll bobbing, smoking contests, races for men and women, climbing greased poles, hunting a pig with a greasy tail, kiss-in-the-ring, dancing etc.'.[6] It was reliably estimated that the total attendance must have neared 20,000.

No rejoicings since have eclipsed this, not even the Victory celebrations of 1945, and the only previous occasion to approach it was the Jubilee of George III in 1809. Hastingers awoke that day to the 'ringing of bells, firing of cannon and music playing'.[7] All the militia and the sea fencibles and the

52 Balloon ascents always attracted good crowds. In 1851 the Duke of Brunswick made a balloon trip from Hastings to Boulogne. A balloon was set up on the evening of 18 August 1825, when the Bourne Street Theatre opened. The same day had seen the opening of Pelham Arcade and the holding of the annual race meeting at Bulverhythe.

53 In the earlier years of the century, Empire Day was taken very seriously. Children saluted the flag and sang patriotic songs and there were impressive processions. The men shown here in 1908 are marching up Queen's Road to Alexandra Park for the main ceremony.

54 Empire Day in the park, seen here in 1909, was a major event in the town's calendar. The day originated as a celebration of Queen Victoria's birthday.

men at the Martello towers fired salutes and after that the soldiers stationed here 'paraded the streets, with the bands playing, colours flying, people huzzaaing etc.' until dinner time.

Then 'upwards of 1000, men and officers, sat down to dinner in the barrack yard on roast beef and plumb pudding'. Meanwhile the mayor and other worthies dined in the Town Hall and the 'poor in the different workhouses feasted on roast beef, plumb pudding and strong beer', a subscription having raised enough to provide 1,850 people with '2880 lbs of beef, 1850 sixpenny loaves, 2880 pints of porter, 2872 gallons of potatoes' and still leave 'a ballance of £188 ... to be distributed amongst 30 of the seamen of Hastings, prisoners of war with France'.

The men and women of the workhouses were also given a shilling each and the children sixpence for them further to enjoy the holiday, and in the evening

> There was a bonfire on the hill, composed of ten waggon-loads of faggots and combustibles, and a tar-barrel on a mast 60 ft. high. Fifty rockets were discharged and many fireworks exhibited. Never let it be said that our forefathers did not known how to enjoy themselves.

As well as such events, there was also the yearly cycle of festivals and fairs to provide full-blooded entertainment. Guizing became the remembrance of Guy Fawkes and during the latter half of the 19th century the many bonfire societies–the three biggest being the St Leonard's, the St Clement's and the Borough societies–paraded the town with their guys. Bands played and the torchbearers vied with each other in the magnificence and imagination of their costumes, until at about 10 o'clock they separated to light their bonfires and set off their fireworks.

Of course, not everybody approved of 'juveniles parading the streets during the day with their "member o'Guy" only once a year'[8] and there were complaints about blocked pavements and boorish behaviour, as well as tart comments to the effect that 'the numerous bands of disturbers of the peace were anything but a credit to the Protestant faith or English commonsense'.[9] Most people, however, thoroughly enjoyed themselves, as they enjoyed the revival of the town's official bonfire celebrations on Hastings Day, 1995.

There was another annual procession on New Year's Day, the 'Rout 'em out' parade that was peculiar to Hastings. In January 1885, London's *Pall Mall Gazette*, speculating on its origins, said that it had been a custom in the town from time immemorial, and described how 'At an early hour the fisherlads parade the old town in a band, and along the East Parade as far as Pelham place, singing in chorus "Rout 'em out, boys; rout 'em out," whereupon oranges, nuts and coppers are thrown out of the windows to be scrambled for'. However, the paper lamented that it had become less fun than in the old days, when it had been customary to heat the coins in an oven before throwing them out. Rout Day even had its own song:

> Rout 'em out, boys; rut 'em out;
> Let the pennnies fly about;
> Today no boats will put to sea,
> Though 'tis fine as fine can be,
> For we'll get a haul on shore
> Worth a last of fish or more.
> Rout 'em out, boys; rout 'em out,
> Let the pennies fly about.

May Day was another great occasion with a troop of dancers and pipers cavorting about Jack-in-the-green, the green being the wickerwork cage covered with evergreens in which he was encased. Then there were the annual fairs. At one time there were five of these, all very ancient and all increasingly disapproved of as the body of the town became more strait-laced and respectable. Fishermen supposedly gambled with golden guineas at the Bulverhythe Fair, and it was alleged that at Rock Fair they 'often staked, and lost, their boats, nets and other appliances'.[10] Toss-ring was the popular gamble at Rock Fair and anyone found cheating was lucky to get away with a ducking in the nearby Priory stream.

55 Judging from their expressions, these schoolchildren of *c.*1909 had mixed feelings about May Day celebrations.

Rock Fair, which possibly dated back to Saxon times, was so called because it was held near the White Rock, and it ran for the two days of 26 and 27 June. The most important of the town's fairs, it was the fishermen's holiday and was said to be 'the only time in all the year when all the fishermen put on their best clothes'.[11] In its later days, it was described as a 'medley of gingerbread, nuts and dolls, Middleton (a form of theatre) and gypsies, peep-shows and penny trumpets, dwarves and giants, gangs and cheapjacks, drinking and dancing'.[12]

As the town expanded into the Priory Valley area, the council was able to squeeze out Rock Fair, which it regarded as 'objectionable and of no benefit', by persuading landowners to deny it a venue in its traditional area. In 1858 it transferred to a field in what is now Manor Road, but could not survive the uprooting and there are no reports of it being held after 1861. Town Fair and Whitsun Fair, held at the Fishmarket on 23 November and Whit Tuesday respectively, soon followed it into oblivion. Declaring them each an 'abominable nuisance', in 1872 the council obtained the consent of the Secretary of State for their abolition, his consent being necessary because they had been established by royal charter. A much smaller fair at Gingerbread Green survived until 1901, when local objections to it, The Green being by then a residential area, were upheld.

56 The pilgrimage from St Mary Star of the Sea to the shrine in the ruins of Hastings Castle was formerly such a tourist attraction that in the 1960s the procession from Old Town was stopped because of the resulting traffic congestion.

CHAPTER FOUR

Expansion and Progress

THE point was made in Chapter One that the early physical history of Hastings almost certainly followed the eastward drift of shingle, with the main settlement of the Hastingers also moving eastwards as the coastline was reshaped. At about the time of the Conquest, or just after, the site of the town became fixed in the Bourne valley and it was not until Hastings began to develop as a watering place and resort in the closing years of the 18th century that it outgrew the valley and spread westward again.

Between 1801 and 1821, its population jumped from 2,982–of whom 2,683 lived in Old Town–to 6,051 as it spread out along the Parade to Wellington Square and towards the Priory Valley. Clearly, people had moved into the town in large numbers. Growth continued throughout the 1820s and in 1828 James Burton began to build his new town of St Leonards a little further along the coast and was very soon able to announce that it was ready to receive its first visitors. The threat of this rival on its doorstep encouraged further development in Hastings and both towns continued to grow and eat up the no-man's-land between them until in 1875 they officially amalgamated to become the County Borough of Hastings and St Leonards.

By then the town definitely centred on the Priory Valley, where the opening of the railway station in 1851 had more-or-less coincided with the development of the Robertson Street area, previously a stretch of wasteland occupied only by ropewalks and the dwellings, ranging from the merest shanties to substantial cottages, of squatters. The Post Office moved from Old Town to Wellington Place in 1854 and then in 1868 to larger premises on the corner of Meadow Road, now Queen's Road.

57 The Welcome Arch was erected at the entrance of Hastings when Princess Victoria and her mother came to stay at St Leonards in 1834. The only route to the new town was through Ore and Hastings, so Burton built a new road from St Leonards to link with the old turnpike road and make access quicker and easier.

58 St Leonards Arch looking west. The arch marked the eastern boundary of Burton's St Leonards. It became a much-loved feature and there was uproar in 1895, when the council had it secretly demolished overnight as a hindrance to traffic.

59 By the end of the 19th century, St Andrew's Arch, the brick tunnel under the railway line at the top of Queen's Road, had become inconvenient and so in 1898 it was dismantled and the tall iron railway bridge was put up in its place.

60 Warrior Square Station, seen here, and Hastings Station were both opened in 1851. Although the former was referred to locally as Gensing Road Station, its official name was always St Leonards; it later became St Leonards Warrior Square to avoid confusion with St Leonards West Marina.

61 Dismantling the Gas Company chimney. When gas making was transferred to Glyne Gap, the old retorts etc. were demolished. When the Gas Company buildings off Queen's Road were erected in 1830, regret was expressed that they 'should be placed where they will be seen so seldom and to such little advantage'.

The Albert Memorial was erected in 1862 on a site where not much more than 20 years before there had been a bridge spanning the Priory stream. In the winter of 1838-9 this stream had been taken underground through an iron pipe and the surrounding marshes and low-lying fields drained to make building possible. By the time the Memorial was built the layout of the town centre was very much as it remained until recent changes consequent upon the demolition of the clock tower in 1973 and the current long-delayed development of Priory Meadow, formerly the Central Cricket Ground, as a shopping centre. Final confirmation that this area had become the business and administrative centre of Hastings came in 1881, when the new Town Hall was built in Queen's Road.

62 *Below left.* At one time Whit-Monday was the only Bank Holiday locally kept. It was Club Day, when all the Friendly Societies first attended church services and then paraded the town with banners flying and bands playing. Servant girls insisted on going home to their villages for Club Day even if they lost their situations through doing so.

63 *Below.* Cambridge Road, looking towards the Memorial. The medieval priory occupied the site of the houses centre left. In 1446, a general pardon for various offences was granted to the prior and all his household–with one exception. That was Eleanor Cobham, who had been found guilty five years before of conspiring with the Witch of Eye and others to kill the king by sorcery so that her husband, the Duke of Gloucester, should succeed him.

64 *Above.* The flooded cricket gound. A picture that unites the present with the past and could even constitute a warning for the future for it is a reminder that the former cricket ground, currently being developed as the town centre shopping complex, was at one time the town harbour, the Priory Haven.

65 Hollington Flats were built in 1965 in the previously semi-rural district of Hollington. They were on the fringes of Ponswood, which had been cleared and made ready for industrial units in 1952. The two developments marked a dramatic change of direction for Hastings.

66 The Town Expansion plan involved clearing most of old Hollington village, a clearance almost as drastic as that previously carried out in the Bourne. The village had developed in the 19th century as terraces of small cottages strung out along the Battle Road.

67 Pelham Crescent, with St Mary in the Castle in the centre, was a speculative venture of the Earl of Chichester. It was designed by Joseph Kay and building began in 1824. During this work a tunnel was discovered leading down from the castle, thus supporting the belief that originally there was a part of the castle at the foot of the cliffs.

Between 1871 and 1881, the population had soared from 29,289 to 42,256. Clive Vale had been laid out by the British Land Company, which had bought the greater part of the land stretching from the Minnis Rock to Ore; Halton had been developed for housing following the pulling down of the barracks in 1823 and the outlying districts of Silverhill, Ore and Hollington had also shown great growth. In the 1850s Silverhill had been looked down upon as a place 'much frequented by the working classes and those destitute of all means of grace', but a little later a number of middle-class villas were put up, mainly for the convenience of prosperous Hastings tradesmen who were abandoning the plebeian habit of living above the shop. Ore, which was absorbed into the County Borough in 1897, and Hollington, part of which was taken into the Borough at the same time as Ore, remained mainly working-class areas and even maintained a semi-rural nature.

Meanwhile, the more fashionable districts of Blacklands and Warrior Square, the Eversfield Estate and Upper St Leonards were also being rapidly developed, with Warrior Square completed in the 1880s. Very soon after that, Hastings and St Leonards, already administratively one town, were made physically one, being united by continuous development along the Sea Front.

It was a remarkable transformation. When Daniel Defoe had visited the town in 1703, he had reckoned that it contained about six hundred buildings; 100 years later, in 1801, when Thomas Pennant 'descended a long steep hill to Hastings, a town crowded in a narrow gap between high hills',[2] the two out-lying parishes of Holy Trinity and St Mary Magdalen still contained only five houses.

Inevitably, the rate of growth meant that builders were often more concerned with getting houses up quickly than with building them well. This was so even in James Burton's prestigious new town of St Leonards, where in February 1829 five houses fell down 'in consequence of the frost and sudden thaw' and had to be rebuilt. There were similar accidents elsewhere and many of the impressive-looking new properties quite soon showed signs of botched workmanship, and by the mid-20th century were adding to the legacy of poor housing in the town.

With the workmen's cottages, the situation was naturally even worse. Few developers took much care with the construction of these; the materials used were poor, facilities were often non-existent and the landlords were reluctant to spend any money on their up-keep, despite charging relatively high rents. Since these cottages were frequently over-crowded–although they were

ANNO SEPTIMO & OCTAVO

GEORGII IV REGIS.

Cap. 22.

An Act to enable Trustees to grant Building Leases of Lands in the several Parishes of *Saint Leonard's Hollington, Saint Mary* of the Castle of *Hastings Maudlin, Saint Mary Magdalen, Saint Michael* near *Hastings,* and *Horsham,* in the County of *Sussex,* Part of the Estates devised by the Will of *Charles Eversfield* Esquire, and to sell the same Lands, and also Two detached Farms in the Parishes of *Hollington* and *Horsham* aforesaid, other Part of the same Estates; and for laying out the Money arising by such Sale in the Purchase of other Estates, to be settled to the same Uses. [14th *June* 1827.]

WHEREAS *Charles Eversfield,* formerly of *Denne Park* in the Parish of *Horsham* in the County of *Sussex,* Esquire, deceased, did, in such Manner as the Law requires for the Validity of Devises of Freehold Estates, duly sign and publish his last Will and Testament in Writing, bearing Date the Seventeenth Day of *March* One thousand eight hundred and eighteen, and thereby devised all those his Manors of *Denn* and *Cheesworth,* and of *Roffey* and *Lea Court,* in the said County of *Sussex,* together with the Rights, Royalties, Members, and

Will of Chas. Eversfield, Esq. dated 17th March 1818.

[*Private.*] 5 *x* Appur-

68 Eversfield Estate Act, 1827. The faith shown by James Burton in his planned new town alerted the Eversfield Estate, which owned virtually all of what became greater St Leonards, to the possibility of development. Hence this Act, which opened the way to speculative building beyond Burton's boundaries.

69 St Leonards at the turn of the century. With the man on horseback riding towards the advancing tram, this picture epitomises the changes and the general speeding up of life in the early years of the 20th century. The electric tramway started operations in 1905, using a stud contact system to avoid unsightly poles and overhead wires along the sea front.

small their occupiers often took in lodgers or even shared with another family in order to pay the rent–the result was that Hastings had areas of slums as bad as those in London or other cities.

The result was a massive housing problem in the 20th century that the authorities long seemed to regard as insoluble. As T.S. Dymond, who was mayor in 1926-7, wrote: 'One of the difficulties to which over-crowding in the town leads is the difficulty of ejecting tenants from houses condemned as unfit for human habitation where no accommodation can be found for them elsewhere'.[3]

The council house building programme embarked upon after the First World War alleviated but did not solve the problem. The first Hastings council houses were at All Saints, Barley Lane and Silverhill. In the '30s further estates were built at Hollington and Red Lake and there was a unique group of steel houses in Clement Hill Road and Fellows Road, an area that became known as Tintown. However, the building programme was not particularly energetic and by September 1939 only 875 units, the majority of them three-bedroomed houses, had been built. After the Second World War there was of necessity a speeded up programme, which included a number of pre-fabs, and in June 1954 no. 62 Blackman Avenue became the 1,000th council house to have been built since the end of the war.

Nevertheless, the housing problem remained and had even worsened. By 1976 there were some 3,000 people on the council waiting list and the older private housing was continuing to deteriorate. A report by Shelter in 1981 stated that 2,800 properties were unfit for human habitation. A further 2,915 lacked basic amenities and 3,500 needed major repairs. It added up to a frightening percentage of the total housing stock, which in 1980 had been put at 31,409 units.

That, of course, is the dark side of the progression from the tiny Hastings described by Defoe. There is also a bright side, with architects such as the Burtons and James Kay producing buildings and groups of buildings of real merit, and lesser men who yet managed a felicity of design that has bequeathed to the town a wealth of treasures and pleasures. There were also benefactors, and even some far-sighted councillors, who ensured that Hastings retained an enviable richness of parks and gardens and open spaces.

In this respect, modern Hastingers owe a debt of gratitude to John Collier, who was the controlling influence in the town, serving as either Town Clerk or Mayor, for a good part of the 18th century. He was the founder of modern Hastings and through his connections with the powerful Pelham family was able to secure for it many benefits and improved amenities. More importantly, the generosity of spirit that he passed on to his descendants has vastly enriched the town. As one local historian has put it:

> He became a great landowner, and, thanks to this, the hills surrounding the town were kept unspoiled by buildings and were ultimately purchased from this successors by the corporation. Part of his fortune was acquired by lending money but this did not limit his outlook and he inaugurated a tradition of generosity where the corporation was concerned which has been continued by his descendants. In recent years, it has been to one of these, Major Carlisle Sayer, that we owe the Firehills and glorious glens to the eastward.[4]

Of the parks and gardens in the town, St Leonards Gardens are the oldest, having been laid out between 1828-30 when Burton was building St Leonards. They were originally subscription gardens for immediate residents and visitors staying at the *St Leonards*, now *Royal Victoria, Hotel*. They were bought by the corporation in 1880.

70 The Tivoli Pleasure Grounds. As the number of visitors increased, so did the demand for more varied entertainment. The *Tivoli Hotel* and Gardens between what is now Battle Road and Sedlescombe Road North became a favourite resort.

TIVOLI NEW ORNAMENTAL GARDENS,

HASTINGS AND ST. LEONARDS.

FIRST GRAND FETE AND GALA will take place on MONDAY next, 13th August. Magnificent display of Fireworks, Rockets, Shells, Mines, Golden Rain and Coloured Fires, concluding with a spectacle, a scene in Macbeth,—witches with boiling caldron of liquid fire.

The gardens briliantly illluminated with many hundred variegated lamps. An additional Band in attendance.

A Montgolfier Balloon will ascend at Six o'clock. Fireworks at half-past Eight.

The Mechanical Exhibition will be lighted up on this occasion.

Admission, 6d. each till Four o'clock; after Four, 1s. Children half-price.

Warrior Square, Wellington Square, Cornwallis Gardens, Linton Gardens, Markwick Gardens and St Matthews Gardens were all originally for subscribers only, as the latter two still are. Warrior Square was acquired by the town in sections; first a strip on the south side of Lower Warrior Square Gardens was bought in 1902 to allow for the erection of the statue of Queen Victoria, the rest of that lower section was bought in 1920, and finally Mr. Holman made a gift of the upper part of the gardens in 1930. Cornwallis Gardens and Amherst Gardens were also gifts in the 1930s, the former being given by Mr. Hedley Williams and the latter by Alderman Thorpe.

The park that has been the longest in public ownership is Gensing Gardens, which was opened in 1872. The site of West Marina Gardens was bought in 1886 but the gardens did not open until 1891. White Rock was bought in 1902 and part of it opened for 'sport and recreation' in 1904 but lack of money delayed the creation of the pleasure grounds until 1920. Linton Gardens was sold to the council in 1937.

The lower part of Alexandra Park, the section south of Park Crossroads, was opened as St Andrew's Gardens in 1864 and was extended to include Newgate and Shornden Woods and the Buckshole Reservoir in 1878. The landscape gardener Robert Marnock, also responsible for Regent's Park Botanical Gardens and Sheffield's Weston Park, was commissioned to design the enlarged park which was officially opened and renamed by the Prince and Princess of Wales on 29 July 1882. In the 1930s there were further enlargements to take in Thorpe Wood and Old Roar Ghyll.

The provision of public recreation grounds in the 20th century has also preserved large areas of open space within the borough, and the purchase of the Summerfields estate not only provided a park-like setting for an embryonic civic centre but also an invaluable stretch of public woodland and a potentially first-class cricket ground. The latter is to be a replacement for the long-time town centre open space, the Central Cricket Ground, or Priory Meadow, which had been first

71 Wellington Square. In the early 1820s the bankers, Breeds, Farncomb and Wenham, financed development on the eastern side of Priory Bridge. This included the *Castle Hotel* and Wellington Square, which by 1824 consisted of 'a double range of very handsome houses, forming two sides of a square, with an oval shaped plantation in front' (Moss). The square was completed in the 1830s.

72 A floral display in Alexandra Park which commemorated the 900th anniversary of the Battle of Hastings. There was a wide range of special events and the day of the battle, 14 October, was adopted as Hastings Day.

73 For many years the Crowning of the May Queen attracted large crowds, whether the ceremony was in Linton Gardens, as shown here, or in Alexandra Park. In recent years, the Jack in the Green Folk Festival has become a major event.

74 Cricket being played at Woodland Vale. London Road can be seen between the hedges and Markwick Terrace is in the distance. Such was the enthusiasm for cricket that it was not unusual for players to get up at 4 a.m. so as to get in as much of a game as possible before starting work at 8 a.m.

75 At the Central Cricket Ground. For the more leisured and affluent, cricket meant the Central Ground in Queen's Road and a match was apt to be as much a social as a sporting occasion.

76 Club House at St Leonards Golf Course. Golf fever infected the leisured classes at about the turn of the century. A nine-hole course was laid out on the East Hill in 1893 and a further nine holes were added in 1896. The St Leonards course was opened in Filsham Park in 1902.

77 Tennis became very popular and in the 1890s there were complaints about the 'lawntennisonians' who made life hazardous on the beach. The group in this photograph is on a private court at Upper St Leonards.

78 The public tennis courts, Central Cricket Ground. An annual open tennis tournament was held at the Central Cricket Ground, which was then a venue for much more than cricket.

proposed as a sports ground in 1861 and had finally opened in 1865.

Contributions to the cost of this ground were made by Viscountess Holmesdale and Countess Waldegrave, the latter of whom played as large a part as anyone in the shaping of Victorian Hastings. She contributed generously to many charities and appeals, built the Bourne Street Wash-houses in 1865 as 'a gift to the poor' and took a close interest in the Hastings Literary and Scientific Institution, which was inaugurated in 1831 and was the forerunner of both the Public Library and the Museum.

What she is chiefly remembered for, though, is the extent to which she contributed to the building funds and endowments of many of the churches built in Hastings during her lifetime, starting with St Clement at Halton in 1838. For this she gave the site, the stone for the building of church, parsonage and school and an endowment of £1,000. Over the next 35 years, she was equally generous in her support of many other such enterprises and in 1861 the drinking fountain in Robertson Street was erected 'In grateful recognition of the constant support afforded by her to the religious and benevolent institutions of the borough and the neighbourhood'. It was paid for by the penny subscriptions of schoolchildren.

It was a well-deserved tribute to a remarkable and public spirited woman but there is no doubt that she was an autocrat and thoroughly enjoyed her position as the uncrowned queen of Hastings, a position secured by her first marriage to Edward Milward the younger and reinforced when on his death she married the Earl of Waldegrave.

Marianne North, the flower painter whose family lived at Hastings, recalled how, when her sister married in 1864, the Countess came close to demanding the right to give away the bride and insisted on making the first speech at the wedding breakfast.[5] As Miss North also remembered the Countess's first husband as the 'Squire of the parish and a despotic magistrate, without whose leave no dog might bark', one feels that the home life of the Milwards must have had some interesting moments.

79 Edward Milward the younger first became mayor in 1785. Between then and 1825 he held that office 20 times, alternating, for a man could not be mayor for two consecutive years, with his father from 1785-1802, with John Goldsworthy Shorter from 1802-16 and with Charles Stevens Crouch from 1816-25. His father, Edward Milward the elder, was mayor 25 times.

There were also moments of more public drama and conflict during that century of hectic growth after the town burst out of the confines of the Bourne valley; the enlargement inevitably meant losses as well as gains and so there was controversy. Infilling had already meant the loss of the gardens going down to the Bourne from All Saints Street and High Street. Then came the friction and uproar of the Crown's claim to the America Ground and the eviction of those who had previously occupied it. Remarkably, some of these moved lock, stock and barrel to the growing St Leonards and there are still cottages there in the Shepherd Street and North Street area that stood originally on the America Ground.

80 White Rock and Cambridge Road in 1840. The area to the left had been occupied by the Ropewalk shown in Powell's map (illustration 82) and also by squatters, who had hoisted the American flag to demonstrate their independence and so earned it the name of America Ground. It was cleared and fenced *c.*1836.

81 *Below left.* Symbolic of a declared intention to look to the future rather than to the past, Marine Court was built in 1937-8, replacing the attractive buildings seen beyond the Arch in illustration 58. Soon known locally as the Skyscraper, it was described by Pevsner as 'the first modernistic affront to the English seaside'.

82 *Below right.* Powell's map of 1822 was published in the third edition of the *Hastings Guide* (1823). It shows the rapid expansion that followed the first move out of the Old Town valley, with Wellington Square and the area east of the Priory Bridge already taking shape. Note the donkey stand opposite what was to become Pelham Crescent.

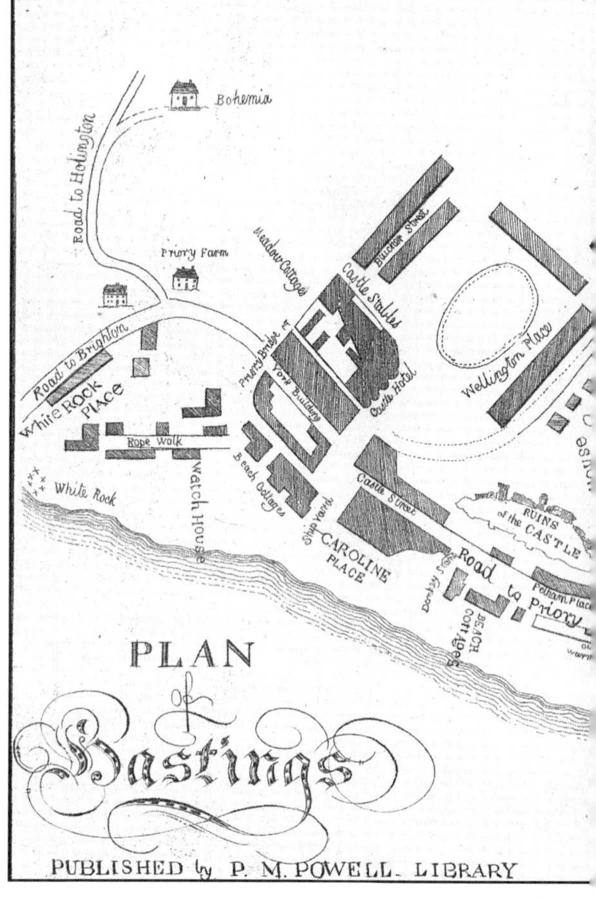

Improvement was always a mixed blessing, though some embraced it wholeheartedly. Writing in 1824, Moss remarked complacently that 'the spirit of improvement and increase of building' meant that there were 'comparatively few old habitations remaining' and that even these were 'gradually disappearing and giving place to erections of a superior class'.[6]

He would, presumably, have applauded the councillors who in 1936 sanctioned the replacement of attractive Regency buildings by the intrusive Marine Court, then the tallest block of flats in the country, which completely upset the line and balance of the sea front. The widely held view that this was cultural vandalism has not been much altered by Marine Court becoming listed as a building of special architectural interest. Still, perhaps by the time that there is no-one left who remembers what it replaced, it will have become more generally treasured.

After all, everyone now rightly values Pelham Crescent and St Mary in the Castle and sees the composite whole as an architectural gem; nobody gives a thought to the fact that the cutting back of the cliffs to allow for its building in 1828 quite severely damaged the castle and its environs. It was much the same when Breeds Place, itself much mourned when it was demolished, was built. Great ropes and teams of oxen were then used to pull down the entire outlying part of the castle grounds known as the Gun Garden to provide the necessary space.

That work was carried out under the supervision of Yorky Smith, who had worked as a young man on the building of the Martello Towers around Pevensey Bay and had come

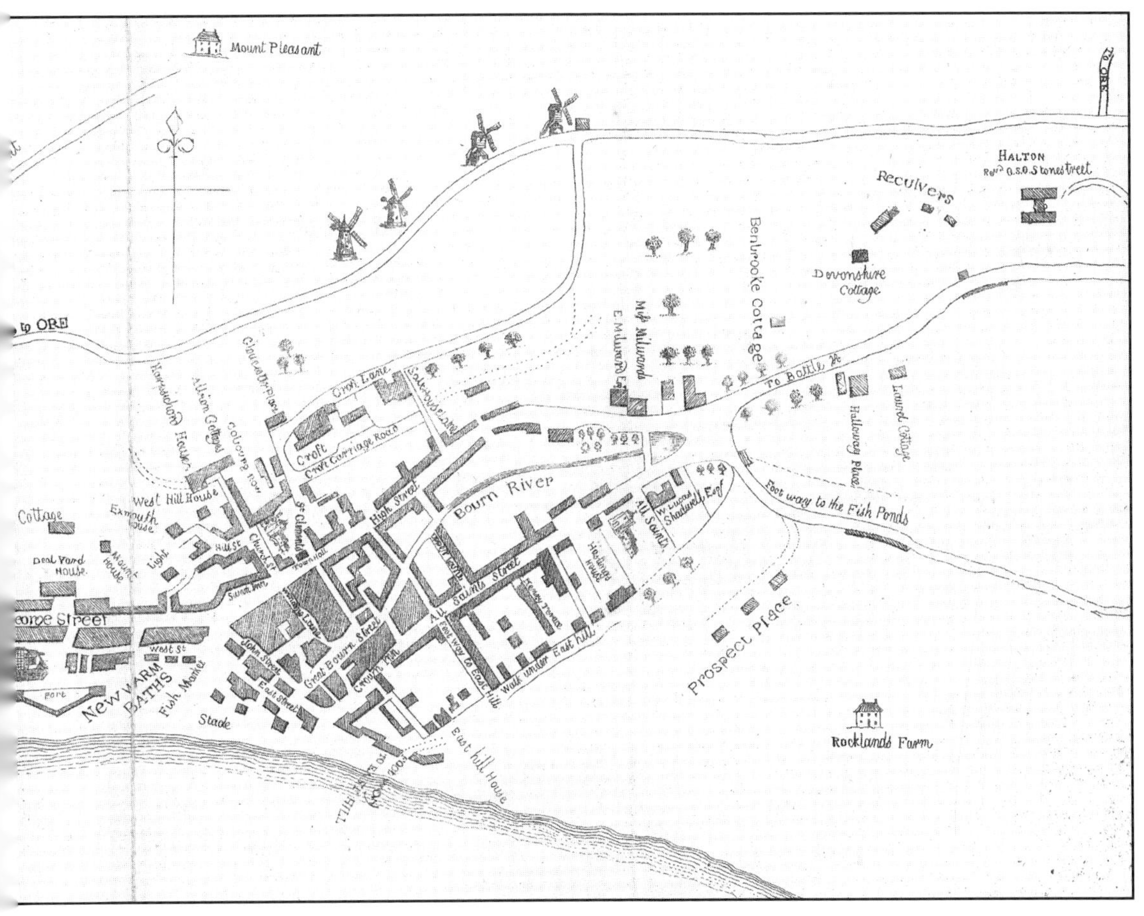

to Hastings *c.*1815. He played an important part in the physical development of Hastings from fishing port to resort. Not only did he build Breeds Place and work for Burton on his St Leonards project but he was also involved in much else, including the building of Wellington Square and of Bohemia House, later renamed Summerfields.

His work for Burton included the construction of 57, Marina, now Crown House. This was the first house to be completed in the new town. The timber framework had been prepared in advance in London and was brought by ship to Hastings and then carried by wagon along to St Leonards, the same procedure that was followed with scaffolding and other materials. The name Crown House was adopted after it had been the home of the Duchess of Kent and Princess Victoria during their stay in 1834.

It is, therefore, of some historical significance for the borough. Nevertheless, it very nearly became yet another lost treasure for by the end of the Second World War it was in a poor state and the councillors eventually who had to decide what should be done about it, evidently did not place much store on historical significance. For them it was merely 'a redundant building of an out-of-date design' and the more cultured of them spoke disparagingly of 'fake Greek architecture'. They decided that it did not merit the protection of being listed.

This was almost on a par with the attitude displayed in 1930 towards the remains of the ancient church of St Mary's, Bulverhythe. The council took over their care, ostensibly to preserve and protect them but promptly cut a road through the site, destroying the foundations of the tower and the nave.

It would seem that then and for a long time afterwards the official policy was overly influenced by the statement made by Sidney Little when he was appointed Borough Engineer in 1926–that the town needed to be dragged into the 20th century. He immediately set out to achieve this end, regardless of history and sentiment. Whether the Concrete King, as he came to be known, was the saviour of modern Hastings or its evil genius is a moot

83 According to Powell's *Hastings Guide* (1823), Caroline Place, 'situated on the Beach near Castle Street, is well defended from the Northern Blast, and commands an excellent view of the sea'. There were six houses, two of which were occupied or owned by Mr. Thos. Thwaites. The shipyard of Thwaites and Winter was close by.

84 Laying the tram tracks caused chaotic disruption for a while, as this scene at the junction of London Road and Norman Road demonstrates. Such confusion was not seen here again until one afternoon in September 1940, when 18 high explosive bombs and an oil bomb were dropped in central St Leonards.

85 The introduction of a public transport system had a marked effect on the town's development but nowhere more so than at Silverhill, which became and remained the depot throughout the progression from trams to trolleys and to motorbuses. It became known as Silverhill Junction or, simply, the Junction.

86 Building the Arterial Road in 1922. Work is in progress on St Helen's Road, or the Arterial Road as it was long designated. It was intended to ease traffic problems and to provide a quick route to the town centre. It also opened up the district to more development.

87 The maids at Summerfields, the school that in 1903 took over the mansion previously known as Bohemia House. Private education was important to the local economy from the early 19th century onwards. In 1923, a local directory listed 43 independent educational establishments in Hastings and St Leonards.

88 St Leonards bathing pool, which opened in 1933, was of Olympic standard and acclaimed as one of the finest in Europe. After the war, it deteriorated and in the 1960s chalets were built around its upper area to convert it into a holiday camp. This closed in the mid-1980s and the site lay derelict until it was cleared in 1993.

DOUBLE DECK PARADE. HASTINGS ~ JUDGES' LTD.

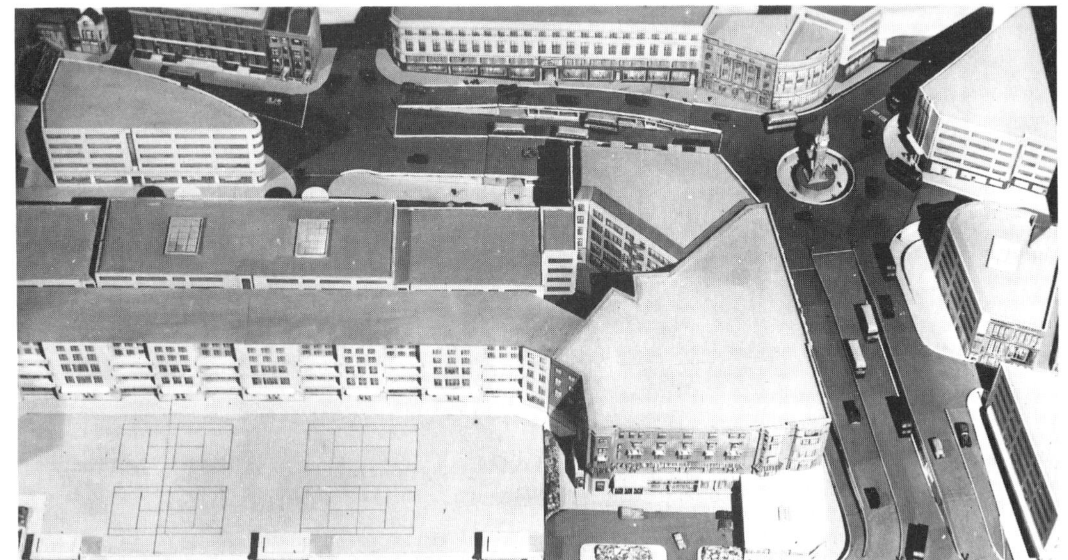

89 *Above left.* Bottle Alley. Sidney Little's transformation of Hastings into a concrete city included the construction in 1933 of the underground promenade, immediately christened Bottle Alley because embedded in the walls was a decorative mosaic of broken glass taken from the rubbish tip.

90 *Above.* A case of the Hastings that might have been. This represents part of the redevelopment plan that Little proposed for the town centre but was never able to proceed with.

91 *Left.* A distinctive feature of central Hastings, were the boats drawn up in front of the *Queen's Hotel*, which disappeared in the early 1930s, when the new promenade, stretching the length of the sea front, was built.

92 While on his way to a service in 1488, the vicar of this church in Hollington was waylaid and robbed by three parishioners. To prevent him testifying against them, they cut out his tongue and pricked his eyes. By what was accepted as a miracle, he recovered sufficient speech and vision to give evidence and his assailants were duly arrested.

point, but he certainly put his mark on the town. He widened and modernised roads, built the new White Rock Baths, the Bathing Pool, Bottle Alley, the modern Promenade and the innovative underground car-parks. He had plans for yet more ambitious schemes that were not realised because of lack of money. But he also provoked a continual furore of controversy.

There were regrets that his extension and widening of the Promenade diminished the town's individuality by taking away the unique feature of boats drawn up to the front of the *Queens Hotel.* More importantly, there was bitter and long-lasting resentment of what seemed almost like a vendetta against the Old Town and the fishing community. The fishermen had to take High Court action to prevent him from clearing them and their boats and net shops away to make room for day trippers and amusements, and the heart was torn out of Old Town by the Bourne Road scheme, involving the compulsory purchase and demolition of great numbers of cottages and small shops.

This was vandalism by any criteria but in the opinion of many it became almost criminal when the ploy of slum clearance was used to obtain the properties at a fraction of what they would have otherwise cost. Owners of houses valued at £3-400 received a derisory £15 or so, and hundreds of Old Towners were moved out to Ore and Hollington.

The clearances started in 1928 but the new road was not completed until 1963. Since then the changes to the town have come thick and fast, causing many to bemoan the passing of the town that they knew and grew up in. Huge new estates, both council and private, have sprung up on what was until recently fields or woodland. Ponswood became an industrial estate in the '50s and 20 years later Hollington was gutted and transformed, with hundreds of acres of countryside around the formerly isolated Church in the Wood covered with shops, factories and a superstore.

Currently, it is the Town Centre that is undergoing a sea change. The Memorial Clock Tower went in 1973, the Council ordering its demolition after an unexplained fire left it allegedly unsafe. Redevelopment, much in the air at that time, has since become a fact, with partial pedestrianisation, a new road structure and the former cricket ground, the one-time site of the town harbour, rapidly taking on a new identity as a shopping complex and car-park.

Chapter Five

Seaside Hastings

THE story of Hastings as a popular seaside resort did not properly begin until the mid-19th century, when the rail links were established with London–via Brighton in 1849, via Ashford and via Tunbridge Wells in 1852. The trains opened up the town to an entirely new type of visitor and brought holiday-makers in previously undreamed of numbers, especially when it became customary, as it very soon did, to run holiday excursions.

There is a note of surprise in the newspaper report of the number who arrived for the Easter holiday of 1865:

> In the course of Thursday the South Eastern Railway Company brought 700 persons into the borough by way of the Tunbridge line alone. The evening express train had an unprecedented number of carriages [20] attached to it, the whole of which were full. A large number of travellers also arrived by the Brighton Company's trains.

93 The seaside paddle; a traditional entertainment that never palled.

TERMS OF SUBSCRIPTION,

At POWELL's Library.

Period.	One Person.	Two Persons.	Three Persons.	Four Persons.	5 or 6 Persons.
	£. s. d.	£. s. d.	£. s. d.	£. s. d.	£. s. d.
A Week	.. 2 6	.. 4 0	.. 5 6	.. 7 0	.. 9 0
Fortnight ..	.. 4 0	.. 7 0	.. 9 0	..10 0	..13 0
One Month .	.. 6 0	..10 0	..13 0	..15 0	..18 0
Two Months	..10 0	..16 0	1 0 0	1 3 0	1 6 0
ThreeMonths	..13 0	1 0 0	1 5 0	1 8 0	1 11 0
Four Months	..15 0	1 4 0	1 10 0	1 15 0	1 18 0
Six Months..	..18 0	1 10 0	1 18 0	2 2 0	2 5 0
Nine Months	1 1 0	1 18 0	2 5 0	2 10 0	2 15 0
One Year ..	1 5 0	2 2 0	2 10 0	2 15 0	3 3 0

Billiard Tables over the Library.

Every information given respecting Lodging Houses.

ON SALE.—JEWELLERY; all sorts of Books, Stationery, and Drawing Books; Camel Hair and other Pencils; Newman's and Ackerman's Colours; Pocket Books; Thread Cases; Cutlery, Knife and Scissar Cases; Tunbridge Ware; Canes and Sticks; Bathing Caps; Perfumery; Snuff, &c.

LET ON HIRE,

At Powell's Library.

Harps Piano Fortes Flutes Violins, and Music	Plate Linen Knives & Forks Sofas and Bath Chairs

94 & 95 An engraving of Powell's Library, *c.*1820 and the subscription terms. Marine libraries and assembly rooms were among the first requirements for a fishing port anxious to turn itself into a fashionable watering place. The first library here opened in 1788; Powell came in 1813.

> There were some very heavy excursions in on Friday, two trains being run by each company. There are reasonable grounds for supposing that there were nearly 4,000 holiday keepers in the town on that day ... In future the South Eastern down excursion trains are not to stop at St Leonards, with a view to avoiding accidents in alighting; the trains have outgrown the length of the platform.[1]

Such crowds were good for business but they occasioned something of a culture shock and there were many locally who bemoaned the passing of the more sedate days, when the town had been a watering place for the gentry, a marine equivalent of such inland spas as Bath and Tunbridge Wells, rather than a holiday resort. These had been the visitors who had set the tone of the place and who had been coming, on the coach or in their own vehicles, since the mid-18th century, and in the 1790s, after Dr. Matthew Baillie, Physician Extraordinary to George III, had begun recommending the recuperative qualities of the Hastings air to his wealthy patients, the numbers had increased sufficiently for the genteel bathing establishments and marine libraries to flourish and for the Assemblies and Balls to be well attended and yet remain select and enjoyable.

In those days, the discriminating recognised it as a place where society 'is gay, without profligacy, and enjoys life, without mingling in its debaucheries' and where there was a pleasing absence of 'professional gamblers, unhappy profligates and fashionable swindlers'.[2] As a local guide book put it, visitors to Hastings would find 'Beauty and fashion ... promenading here in the summer evening'.[3]

There may have been some local resentment that Dr. Baillie had not sent the king to Hastings for his salt-water treatments but the patients to whom he did recommend the town were of a pleasing station in life and

96 *The Warrior's Gate.* For many years, Hastings was quite notorious for the number of pubs and beer-houses relative to its population. In the 1930s there was a campaign to cut the number. When the Chief Constable unsuccessfully opposed the renewal of *The Swan*'s licence, he declared that there were 12 other pubs within 100 yards of it and 26 within 400 yards.

the town prospered accordingly. Nor was royal patronage entirely lacking. George III's son, Prince Augustus Frederick, spent the summer of 1794 here, staying with his wife and son at East Hill House, Tackleway, and the Duke of Cumberland and his family stayed at Breeds Place in 1833. During their stay, Prince George laid the foundation stone of the George Street Market Hall and launched a ship from the local yards. There was also the prolonged stay, about which so much has been written, of the Princess Victoria and her mother, from 5 November 1834 to 29 January 1835, and Queen Adelaide spent the winter of 1837 at 23, Grand Parade, later renamed Adelaide House in her honour.

It was not surprising that many looked back on those pre-railway days as a sort of lost golden age, but, unfortunately, such nostalgia developed into a town characteristic and had a lot to do with Hastings failing to maintain and capitalise on the head start that it had enjoyed over most other resorts.

In 1851 it had been the fourth largest resort in the country, its population of 17,621 exceeded only by those of Brighton (65,569), Great Yarmouth (26,880) and Dover (22,244), and of these the latter two were 'inflated by non-resort elements'.[4] By 1881, its population had jumped to 42,258 and the only larger resort was Brighton (107,546). After that, it lost ground in terms of both size and appeal. It was overtaken in point of population first by Bournemouth and Southend and then by others, and the wealthier visitors increasingly found newer resorts more attractive.

Even when the council finally accepted, in the 1920s, that positive steps had to be taken to halt the town's decline, it was still not able to yield completely to the realities of the holiday industry. While it was agreed that the way forward had to include catering for the more popular end of the market and for day-trippers, there remained a desperate desire that this should be done in such a way as not seriously to damage the town's

97 This postcard dates from 1914, when the Joy Wheel at the shore end of the pier was enormously popular. For many local diehards, it was a sign of the increasing vulgarisation of the pier and of the resort.

SWAN HOTEL,

COMMERCIAL & POSTING HOUSE,

HIGH STREET.

Wines of superior quality.

W. Carswell

In soliciting a continuance of that patronage which the above Hotel has enjoyed for the last 50 years, begs to assure its frequenters that no exertion on his part shall be spared to ensure every comfort and luxury, combined with the most moderate charges, to those who may honour him with their commands.

THE STABLING

Immediately contiguous to the house is most extensive and convenient. Saddle Horses for Ladies and Gentlemen, Post Chaises, Landaulette, Barouche, &c., on the shortest notice.

COACHES DAILY

To LONDON, BRIGHTON, DOVER, &c.

98 These hotel advertisements appeared in the 1880s. By then, the railway was bringing in large numbers of middle-class visitors throughout the summer and Bank Holiday crowds filled the town to over-flowing. Nevertheless, it is clear that Hastings hankered after gentility.

complacent and rather snobbish self-image.

Consequently, a compromise policy was devised whereby the coach parties and the amusements, all the candy floss and kiss-me-quick aspects of the seaside were to be concentrated in the Old Town area, leaving the rest of Hastings and St Leonards as the preserve of the more sedate and respectable longer-stay visitors upon whom the hoteliers, who then exerted a great deal of influence, depended. Officially, it was considered 'good policy to concentrate the more gregarious forms of entertainment at one end of the town and to retain at the other end the quiet character which is more agreeable to the longer term visitor'.[5]

Broadly speaking, the segregation of the day-trippers remained the policy even when it eventually had to be accepted that the traditional hotel and boarding house visitors were no longer coming to the town in significant numbers. It was certainly still strongly in place in 1945, when the council threw out proposals from their planning consultant designate that the Stade area should be restored to the fishermen and that trippers should be directed westwards.

The author of the report was sacked and Sidney Little was given the additional job of Town Planning and Development Officer. He immediately came up with an ambitious scheme that would have meant the total sacrifice of the fishing quarter to produce a Hastings holiday enclave. His plan included a giant amusement park to the east of the boating lake and an extension of the promenade that would take it alongside a lagoon to Ecclesbourne.

The council actually approved this scheme but the combination of a public outcry and a shortage of money prevented its implementation. However, subsequent

99 The beach near Robertson Street in 1909. From late-Victorian times onwards, a photographic memento of the seaside holiday became a 'must' and so the beach photographer became ubiquitous. The photographs were developed on the spot in a portable 'darkroom'.

100 Pleasure boats at Breeds Place. As well as the organised trips, boats of all sizes were available for personal hire. Towards the end of the 19th century, it cost 10s. an hour to hire a sailing boat 30ft. or more in length and 5s. for one under 30ft.; a rowing boat cost 2s. 6d.

decisions showed that the underlying philosophy regarding holiday-makers remained substantially unchanged since the 1930 Development Plan.

To be fair to the council, its inability to shrug off old attitudes and to make a genuinely whole-hearted response to changing trends reflected the general mood of the town. This remained, as it had done for a hundred years or more, a nostalgic yearning for past glories.

In 1864, a Sea Front resident complained:

> It is well known that Sunday after Sunday, during the summer months of last year, parties were bathing in front of some of the best properties in the borough till one, and frequently two o'clock in the afternoon, and I can testify that scenes of a disgraceful character were often witnessed. The practice, I am satisfied, is most offensive to visitors, and, if continued, will prove injurious to the town ... The parties who bathe at so late an hour on Sunday, and find delight in indulging in acts of indecency, are excursionists who come into the town for the day only, and not those visitors who make a more lengthened stay amongst us.[6]

Over a century later, a lady born in 1907 and who had had what would nowadays probably be described as a deprived childhood, regarded the changes in holiday-makers with regret and recalled that in her young days, 'There were different types of tourist in Hastings ... the summer visitors and also the winter visitors of good quality. The *Victoria Hotel* was always full of people in the winter. But it was also a good class of summer visitor. Not quite the day tripper type. They'd bring their families and take a house for a month.'[7]

There had been a time when this taste for decorum and the eschewing of the more vulgar aspects of the seaside had worked to Hastings' advantage. Indeed, in one important aspect of public decency it had at one time been held up as an example to other resorts. The writer of a letter to the *Scarborough Gazette* in 1851 declared: 'If the correspondent in your last week's paper signed 'A Visitor' had, when at Brighton, extended his visit to Hastings, he would have seen there in practice a very simple remedy for the evils of which he complains; no gentleman there is allowed to bathe without a pair of drawers.'[8]

What that writer did not know was that the regulation had aroused opposition at Hastings from those who did not like the new ideas and attitudes that were shaping the town. As late as 1850, the police had trouble with a group of men who made mock of the bye-law by bathing with their drawers around their necks instead of their loins and, rather surprisingly, the magistrates dismissed the subsequent prosecution. Inspector Campbell was told very brusquely that the police had no right to be so intrusive and officious and that it would have served them right had they been given a good ducking.

However, conformist respectability soon triumphed over sturdy independence and, throughout the second half of the century and beyond, bathing regulations were rigorously enforced. Men and women bathed from separate beaches with their bathing machines kept a prescribed distance apart. Mixed bathing was not allowed until 1903, two years after the neighbouring resort of Bexhill had acquired some notoriety by pioneering this relaxation of Victorian mores.

It was a watershed decision, serving almost as official confirmation that Hastings was no longer a watering place but had become a fully fledged seaside pleasure resort. The health angle continued to be stressed in the town's publicity and doctors continued to recommend its curative properties, but letting friends and families relax on the beach together and swim together was acknowledgement of what had long been true in fact–that people came to the seaside to enjoy themselves and that the beach was central to that enjoyment.

For much of the 19th century, this had certainly not been the case. The sea had been valued only for its curative properties and the entertainments on offer had been the sugar to coat the unpalatable pills of the copious draughts of sea water that the doctors prescribed and the controlled dippings, total immersions in the water, carried out by the bathing machine attendants.

A dipping had little in common with pleasure. The lumbering, high-wheeled horse-drawn bathing machine was drawn into the water and the bather was seized by the shoulders and plunged vigorously under the water the number of times prescribed by the doctor. The superior machines were fitted with a modesty hood that spread out almost to the surface of the water to provide total privacy.

The various bathing establishments in both Hastings and St Leonards were popular not only because few of the lodging houses had facilities for baths but also because they did away with the need to go through the undignified process of being dipped. There was so much faith in the medical qualities of sea-water that the Baths also did a brisk morning trade supplying buckets of it, hot or cold, to lodging houses and private homes at a charge of 3d. or 4d. a bucket. In St Leonards, some of the gentry actually had a salt-water supply connected to their homes, their baths being fitted with a third tap for it.

Nevertheless, the use of the machines 'for bathing in the open sea' increased steadily and by the mid-century bathers could choose from Cobby's machines 'at the Marine-parade, and near Caroline-place, Hastings; Dunn's, at the corner of Carlisle-parade; Robinson and Oliver's, Eversfield-place; and French's, at St Leonards'.[9] The owners paid the council an annual rent of 1s. for each machine and this was collected by the Pier Warden 'on the 25th day of December, yearly'.

By the mid-century, many gentlemen had reclaimed the freedom to swim rather than merely to be dipped, but this uncontrolled bathing resulted in a number of accidents and so in 1855 the council provided 'drags, ropes, a boat, and the attendance of a man at the East Groyne, White Rock Groyne, and other places along the beach'.[10] It could claim, therefore, to have been one of the first resorts to employ lifeguards.

However, the more timid men and virtually all women continued for a long time to rely upon the attendants and as late as 1937 a local publication recorded that 'Personal recollections still linger of that kindly autocrat of the beach, the bathing woman in the poke bonnet and ample skirt without whose assistance none but the most determined ladies were able to bathe'.[11]

The machines outlasted the dippers because they continued to be essential as changing rooms, but the end for them was signalled in 1906, when one of the concessionaires, Ben Laws, finding that alterations to the Parade made it difficult to move his machines out of danger in rough weather, replaced a number of them with the canvas changing cabins that were in use at some of the continental resorts. He claimed that his were the first such cabins to come into use in this country.

Their superiority over the bathing machines was soon realised and there were soon large numbers of them on the Hastings beaches. Even so, there were not enough to cope adequately with the rocketing numbers of swimmers in the years following the introduction of mixed bathing. Consequently, the council had to take another great step out of the Victorian past and relax the rules of the beach to allow 'macintosh bathing'. This meant that an intending bather could go to the beach ready changed but with a macintosh, or something similar, on over his or her costume. After a swim and perhaps a drying off in the sun, the macintosh went on again and the bather returned home or to an hotel room to get dressed.

This proved, as Mrs. Grundy and her relatives had grimly forecast, to be the thin end of the wedge that resulted soon enough in the free-for-all of changing on the beach, with much wriggling about under strategically placed towels, and finally, in 1977, permission given for a beach at Fairlight to be opened up for nude bathing.

Not that such modern licence was envisaged in the early 1900s. Even macintosh bathing did little enough at first

101 This postcard epitomises the Edwardian seaside. It has it all; the crowded beach, Punch and Judy, bathing machines and changing huts and, in the distance, the pleasure yacht, *Albertine.*

to free the beaches. The official bathing stations remained and for many years macintosh bathers continued to be charged 3d. for the privilege of using the beach. For more conventional beach users, it cost an adult 6d. a bathe to hire a changing tent, while a child under 14 paid 3d. For those who were either economically-minded or very keen swimmers, a small saving could be made by buying a book of a dozen tickets. It was also quite usual to hire costumes, caps, sand shoes and towels. It cost 2d. per item for the costume, cap and shoes, and 1d. for the towel.

Despite the charges and the regulations and the town's determination to remain 'good class', by the turn of the century the pattern of what is now seen as the traditional seaside holiday was well established. Photographs of the period show crowded beaches and, although to modern eyes the holiday-makers appear very formally and soberly dressed, they are clearly enjoying themselves.

Both on and off the beaches there were what the local directories of the '90s termed 'al fresco entertainments'–the sand artists and Punch and Judy, itinerant musicians, the 'recitator with his blood-curdling narrative' and the fortune tellers with their little birds that picked out the roll of paper that would reveal the enquirer's future; and everywhere there were the photographers, eager to provide a permanent reminder of how good it had been at the seaside.

102 The beach at Hastings, *c.*1907. The promenade and beach of Edwardian Hastings presented a façade of quiet prosperity and decorous enjoyment but behind the frontline was Mugsborough, the town depicted in Tressell's *Ragged Trousered Philanthropist*, where many experienced extremes of poverty and hardship.

BOVRIL

103 *Above.* Sand artists, termed sand scratchers locally, produced masterpieces, using wire tools rather like toasting forks. They dug trenches around their pictures to protect them from the water. Sand building competitions were very popular.

104 *Below left.* Beach entertainers–Punch and Judy men, minstrels, pierrots, buskers of all sorts–were numerous and drew appreciative audiences both from the beach and from the promenade above.

105 *Below right.* The lemonade seller was a welcome sight on the beach on a hot summer's day.

There was also the ever-present sound of music, which had been a feature of seaside life from its earliest days, when concerts were provided at which visitors could 'hear the dulcet tones of some sweet syren and list with pleasure to music's fascinating pipe'.[12] From 1829 onwards, the Town Band played from a stage erected against the wall of Marine Parade and by the 1870s this had been augmented by a German Band under the direction of Herr Kluckner.

Top-class artistes, including Charles Halle, Madame Patti, Clara Butt and Paderewski appeared at the Music Hall, which was later renamed the Public Hall, and at the Royal Concert Hall, built in 1876 just north of Warrior Square. When Hastings Pier opened in 1872 and St Leonards Pier in 1891, they initially sought to follow this tradition. *Pike's Directory* for 1889 pointed out that on Hastings Pier it cost only 2d. to enjoy

> the performance of a first-rate orchestral band, supplemented by vocal music of like character' and promised that the proposed St Leonards Pier would also offer only 'select entertainment'.

However, the growing demand for a more robust type of music also had to be catered for. Come the 1880s, a visitor, Mrs. McLelland, paid for a bandstand to be put

106 Fred Judge started producing local postcards in Hastings in 1904 and became one of the most famous of all the postcard photographers. A photograph taken in 1904 of 'Lightning on Hastings Pier' became an instant best-seller, with 25,000 of the cards bought within the year. He died in 1950 at 78 years of age. There are now many specialist collectors of his cards.

107 & 108 Hastings pier, *above*, St Leonards pier, *below*. The building of Hastings pier in 1872 and St Leonards pier in 1891 heralded the arrival of what became the traditional seaside holiday. At first sedate promenades, they developed into increasingly brash entertainment centres. St Leonards pier, badly damaged by fire, never re-opened after the Second World War and its remains were cleared away in 1951.

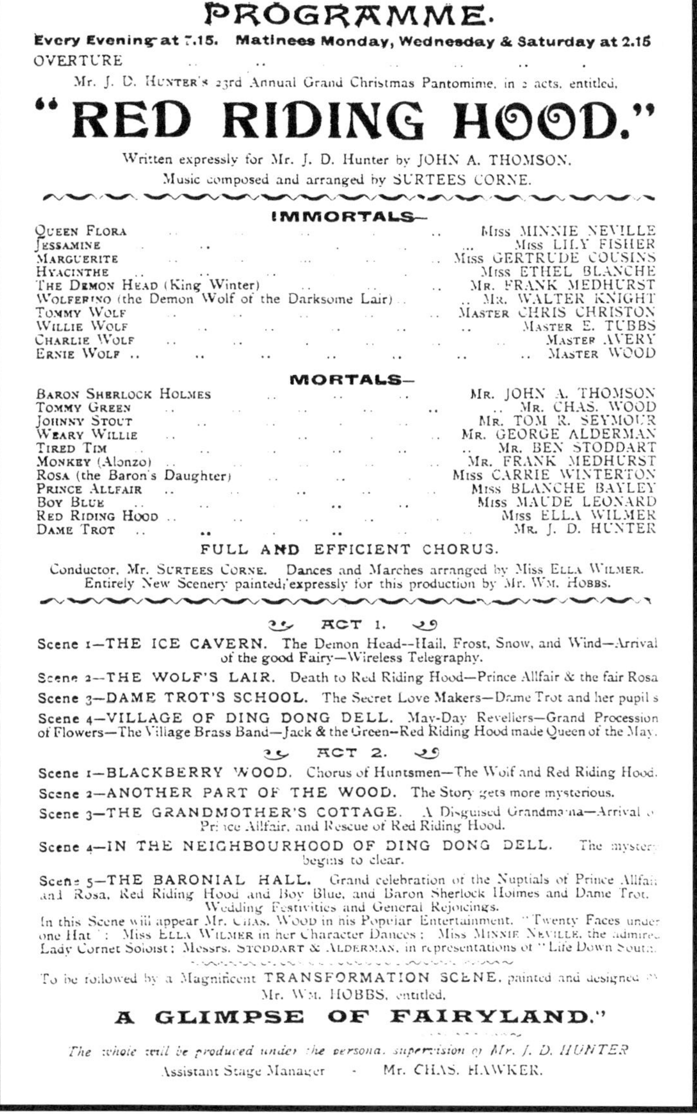

PROGRAMME.

Every Evening at 7.15. Matinees Monday, Wednesday & Saturday at 2.15

OVERTURE .. ..

Mr. J. D. HUNTER's 23rd Annual Grand Christmas Pantomime, in 2 acts, entitled,

"RED RIDING HOOD."

Written expressly for Mr. J. D. Hunter by JOHN A. THOMSON.

Music composed and arranged by SURTEES CORNE.

IMMORTALS—

QUEEN FLORA	Miss MINNIE NEVILLE
JESSAMINE	Miss LILY FISHER
MARGUERITE	Miss GERTRUDE COUSINS
HYACINTHE	Miss ETHEL BLANCHE
THE DEMON HEAD (King Winter)	MR. FRANK MEDHURST
WOLFERINO (the Demon Wolf of the Darksome Lair)	MR. WALTER KNIGHT
TOMMY WOLF	MASTER CHRIS CHRISTON
WILLIE WOLF	MASTER E. TUBBS
CHARLIE WOLF	MASTER AVERY
ERNIE WOLF	MASTER WOOD

MORTALS—

BARON SHERLOCK HOLMES	MR. JOHN A. THOMSON
TOMMY GREEN	MR. CHAS. WOOD
JOHNNY STOUT	MR. TOM R. SEYMOUR
WEARY WILLIE	MR. GEORGE ALDERMAN
TIRED TIM	MR. BEN STODDART
MONKEY (Alonzo)	MR. FRANK MEDHURST
ROSA (the Baron's Daughter)	MISS CARRIE WINTERTON
PRINCE ALLFAIR	MISS BLANCHE BAYLEY
BOY BLUE	MISS MAUDE LEONARD
RED RIDING HOOD	MISS ELLA WILMER
DAME TROT	MR. J. D. HUNTER

FULL AND EFFICIENT CHORUS.

Conductor, Mr. SURTEES CORNE. Dances and Marches arranged by Miss ELLA WILMER.
Entirely New Scenery painted expressly for this production by Mr. WM. HOBBS.

ACT 1.

Scene 1—THE ICE CAVERN. The Demon Head—Hail, Frost, Snow, and Wind—Arrival of the good Fairy—Wireless Telegraphy.

Scene 2—THE WOLF'S LAIR. Death to Red Riding Hood—Prince Allfair & the fair Rosa

Scene 3—DAME TROT'S SCHOOL. The Secret Love Makers—Dame Trot and her pupils

Scene 4—VILLAGE OF DING DONG DELL. May-Day Revellers—Grand Procession of Flowers—The Village Brass Band—Jack & the Green—Red Riding Hood made Queen of the May.

ACT 2.

Scene 1—BLACKBERRY WOOD. Chorus of Huntsmen—The Wolf and Red Riding Hood.

Scene 2—ANOTHER PART OF THE WOOD. The Story gets more mysterious.

Scene 3—THE GRANDMOTHER'S COTTAGE. A Disguised Grandmamma—Arrival of Prince Allfair, and Rescue of Red Riding Hood.

Scene 4—IN THE NEIGHBOURHOOD OF DING DONG DELL. The mystery begins to clear.

Scene 5—THE BARONIAL HALL. Grand celebration of the Nuptials of Prince Allfair and Rosa, Red Riding Hood and Boy Blue, and Baron Sherlock Holmes and Dame Trot. Wedding Festivities and General Rejoicings.

In this Scene will appear Mr. CHAS. WOOD in his Popular Entertainment, "Twenty Faces under one Hat": Miss ELLA WILMER in her Character Dances: Miss MINNIE NEVILLE, the admired Lady Cornet Soloist: Messrs. STODDART & ALDERMAN, in representations of "Life Down South."

To be followed by a Magnificent TRANSFORMATION SCENE, painted and designed by Mr. WM. HOBBS, entitled,

"A GLIMPSE OF FAIRYLAND."

The whole will be produced under the personal supervision of Mr. J. D. HUNTER

Assistant Stage Manager - Mr. CHAS. HAWKER.

109 Johnny Hunter's pier pantomime was long a tradition in the town. He was appointed Entertainments Manager in 1879 and put on the first of his pantomimes at Christmas of that year. The complete show, including, scenery, costumes and cast, cost £20 a week to put on.

up near Hastings Pier and the tradition of outdoor band concerts was soon firmly established. Further bandstands went up, including ones at Warrior Square, in Alexandra Park and, later, in White Rock Gardens, and listening to the band became a favourite entertainment of visitors and residents alike.

The Scots Band engaged each year prior to the First World War to play at St Leonards Pier was particularly popular, even to the point of inspiring impromptu dancing on the Promenade. This, though, was rather frowned upon and eventually the band was shut off from the non-paying 'hoi polloi'.

Meanwhile, the constantly growing taste for other types of entertainment also had to be satisfied. Both piers quite soon became noted for variety shows and regular seasons of plays, and before the end of the century even the Royal Concert Hall was billing such artistes as Albert Chevalier and George Robey. The Gaiety Theatre, built on the site of old stables opposite the Town Hall, opened

110 The town's first bandstand was built near the baths in 1883 and was the gift of a Mrs. McLelland, a regular visitor. In the 1890s, the town was permitted to impose a farthing rate to pay for the band.

111 In 1918, Wallis Arthur's Concert Party performed every evening at 8 o'clock in the Central Pavilion at the Cricket Ground, and every afternoon at 3.15 at the Alexandra Park bandstand. If it was wet, the afternoon performance was transferred to the Cricket Ground Pavilion. Seat prices were 5d., 9d. and 1s. 6d., including tax.

in 1882 with a D'Oyly Carte production of 'HMS Pinafore' and in 1899 the Hippodrome was built on Marine Parade as a music-hall theatre where Marie Lloyd, who topped the bill on the opening night, and her fellow performers provided entertainment to match the cheerful vulgarity of the theatre's architecture.

In addition, there were the ever-popular minstrels, firm favourites locally since 1865, when the original Christy's troupe performed in the town and inspired a number of local amateurs to put on the burnt cork and white gloves to raise money for various charities. Soon, there were minstrel pitches by what became the boating lake, where the stage surround was made up of old railway sleepers, and near the *Queen's Hotel*, where the company performed in front of a flat board and lingered long in local memory because the accompaniment was provided by a very large man playing a very small harmonium.

112 The Swanee Minstrels, often referred to as the Ethiopians, were for many years *the* popular entertainers. Those who performed on the beach or elsewhere in the open were dependent on the speed and the patter of their bottler (collector) to get a good return for their efforts.

113 The Peerless Pierrots. At about the turn of the century, the minstrels began to lose ground to the pierrots. As with the minstrels, a pierrot show might mean a performance on the pier or in a theatre or a less sophisticated venue such as an outdoor pitch or on the beach.

114 Ye Merrie Folke Concert Party. Pierrots developed into concert parties. With this group, one can only hope that their material showed more inspiration than their choice of name.

115 The Blind Street Musicians were for some years amongst Hastings' most popular street entertainers.

116 King's Road put on a colourful welcome display when the Prince of Wales visited in 1927. The road was built as a residential street rather than a commercial one and was known originally as Gensing Station Road.

The famous Mohawk and Moore and Burgess troupes, each about forty strong, often appeared at local theatres and the Mohawks had a regular month-long season at St Leonards Pier. Coincidentally, the final performance of the Moore and Burgess troupe, before it amalgamated with the Mohawks, was at St Leonards Pier on 16 June 1900.

After that, the appeal of the minstrels waned and it was the turn of the pierrots, until their distinctive costumes began to stamp them as old-fashioned and they evolved into more sophisticated concert parties and resident summer shows. Of these, the ones most closely associated with Hastings were the Fol-de-Rols and Clarkson Rose's 'Twinkle'. The Fol-de-Rols were booked for the opening season of the White Rock Pavilion in 1926 and remained the resident summer show until the outbreak of the Second World War. After the war, Clarkson Rose had a long run there.

In the 1940s and '50s and thereon, the years between the wars became the lost golden age that the town harked back to, a time of innovation and enterprise, of progress and profit. In truth, though, 25 years of undeniably impressive effort had not enabled the town to recover its top-ranking among the resorts; they had merely temporarily halted its decline. As D. Robert Elleray has pointed out, between 1900 and 1950 Worthing upped its population from 22,567 to 69,431, whereas the comparable figures for Hastings showed a drop from 65,556 to 65,522.[13]

For a few short years after the war, it almost seemed as if the decline had been halted and the great days were returning. Visitors, starved of holidays and entertainment for years, flocked into the town in such numbers that, in cases known to the writer, families of those who did 'summer lets' had to sleep on the floor to release their beds.

FISHERMEN'S HEARTY WELCOME
TEA
COFFEE
& COCOA
ESTABLISHED

117 When the Prince of Wales arrived for the opening of the White Rock Pavilion, 1927, the Old Town was particularly enthusiastic about his visit and celebrated in some style. Like most distinguished visitors, he was made a member of the Winkle Club.

118 In the early days it saved time and was a lot less expensive to photograph groups of people rather than individuals and the *Albertine*, the most famous of the local pleasure yachts, provided a favourite setting. The low shutter speeds meant that movement produced 'ghosts'.

It proved, though, but a brief Indian summer of success, masking the fact that the town's career as a seaside resort was all but over. The pleasure yachts, the *Albertine* and the *Skylark*, had become but a distant memory, the steamships that had provided trips to Boulogne and the Isle of Wight had mostly been sunk during the war and an attempt to revive the service was short-lived. St Leonards Pier had ended the war a ruin, having been gutted by fire, and its ugly remains were cleared away. With the exception of the White Rock Pavilion, the theatres had long since been converted into cinemas, though variety entertainments continued for a while at the De Luxe and Regal. Once the television era began, it was not long before the cinemas closed. Now there is only one left where not so long ago there were eight.

The Pier Theatre, which had for years housed a resident repertory company–the Court Players–closed with the rest and various other enterprises, including a small zoo on the Parade extension at the entrance to the Pier, proved short-lived.

The number of hotels dropped steadily, many of them converted into flats or nursing

119 Dick Russell's charabanc trips. Charabancs and waggonettes took late 19th- and early 20th-century holiday-makers for drives to beauty spots and tea gardens. Children, laying in wait at spots where hills slowed the drive out of town, won pennies and halfpennies by performing cartwheels etc. behind the vehicles. They called this waggonetting.

DICK RUSSELL,

RIDING ✠ AND ✠ JOB ✠ MASTER,

ST. ANDREW'S MEWS,

QUEEN'S ROAD, HASTINGS.

HORSES AND TRAPS OF EVERY DESCRIPTION.

SADDLE HORSES & QUIET PONIES

For Ladies and Children on Hire.

Station Orders punctually attended to. Horses on Job by Day, Week, Month or Year.

THE ✠ "RELIANCE,"

Superior New 4-Horse Char-a-Banc will run as under :

RETURN FARES—

MONDAYS, Winchelsea & Rye	4/-	THURSDAYS, Bodiam Castle	4/6
TUESDAYS, Battle Abbey and Normanhurst	4/-	FRIDAYS, Hurstmonceux ,,	5/-
WEDNESDAYS, Country Drive	2/-	SATURDAYS, Country Drive	2/-
		Intermediate Trips to Fairlight	1/6

Private Parties & Beanfeasts at Reduced Prices. Horses bought & sold on commission.

Orders and Seats booked at St. Andrew's Mews, Queen's Road. Also at King's Road Mews, King's Road, St. Leonards.

Private Residence—1, STOCKLEIGH ROAD, ST. LEONARDS.

120 A hovercraft, based here in 1966, proved a very short-lived successor to the pleasure steamers which operated from Hastings Pier from the 1880s to the beginning of the Second World War and for a short time afterwards. Pre-1914, a trip to Boulogne and back, allowing 3½ hours ashore, cost 5s.

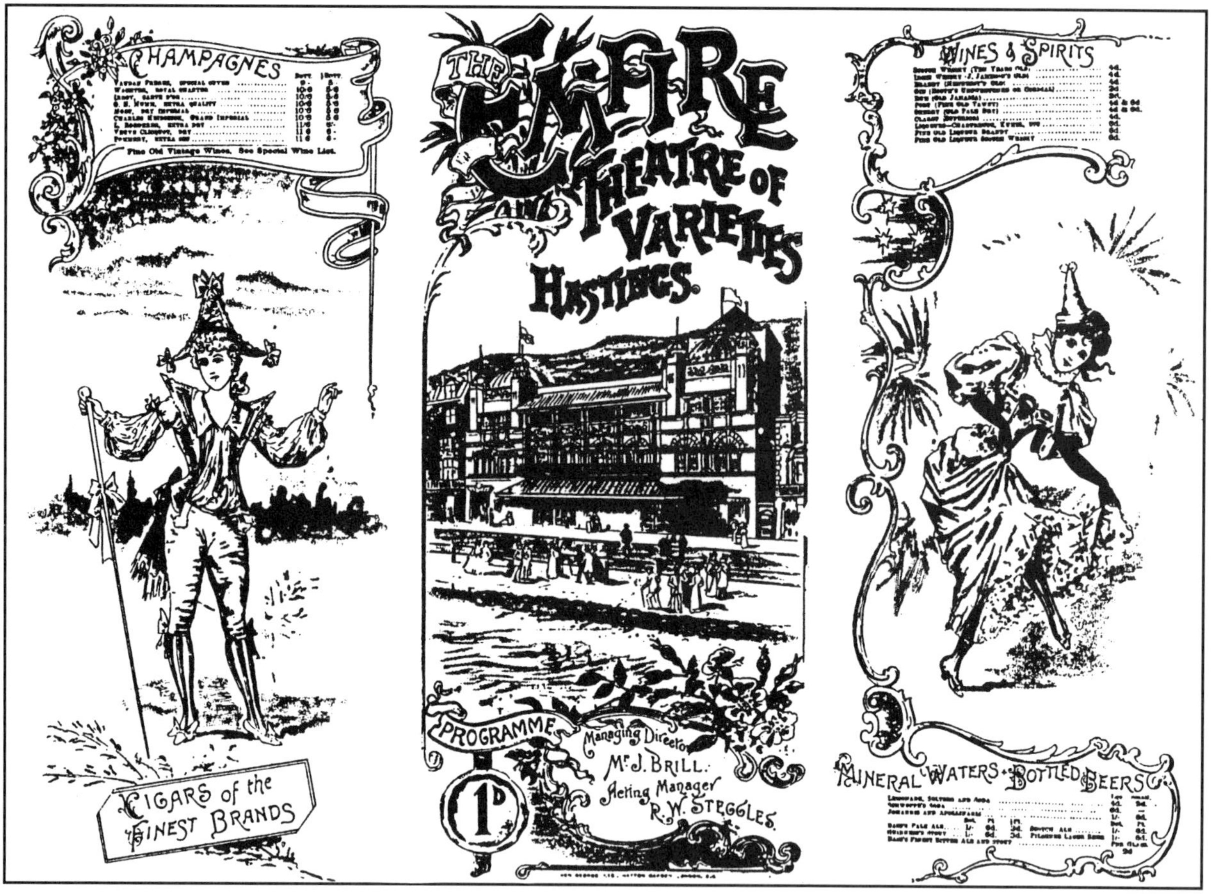
CHAMPAGNES
Fine Old Vintage Wines. See Special Wine List.
CIGARS of the FINEST BRANDS
THE EMPIRE THEATRE OF VARIETIES HASTINGS.
PROGRAMME
1D
Managing Director Mr J. BRILL.
Acting Manager R. W. STEGGLES.
WINES & SPIRITS
MINERAL WATERS & BOTTLED BEERS

121 The Empire Theatre. This became the Empire Theatre of Varieties in 1901, two years after it had opened as the Marine Palace of Varieties. The name changed again, to the Hippodrome, in 1905 and in 1910 it was converted into the Royal Cinema de Luxe. This title was shortened to the Cinema de Luxe in the 1920s. It closed as a cinema on 24 July 1965.

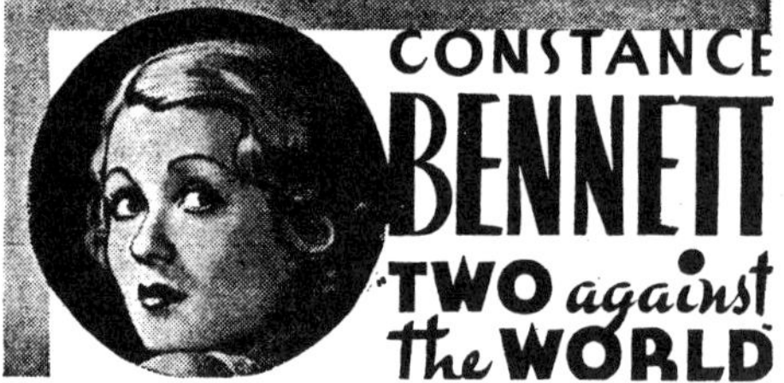

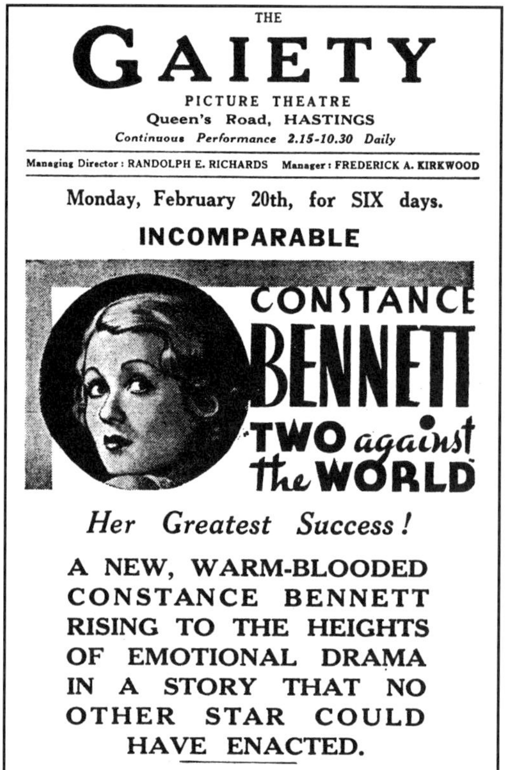
THE
GAIETY
PICTURE THEATRE
Queen's Road, HASTINGS
Continuous Performance 2.15-10.30 Daily
Managing Director: RANDOLPH E. RICHARDS Manager: FREDERICK A. KIRKWOOD
Monday, February 20th, for SIX days.
INCOMPARABLE
CONSTANCE
BENNETT
TWO against the WORLD
Her Greatest Success!
A NEW, WARM-BLOODED CONSTANCE BENNETT RISING TO THE HEIGHTS OF EMOTIONAL DRAMA IN A STORY THAT NO OTHER STAR COULD HAVE ENACTED.
FULL SUPPORTING PROGRAMME.

122 Advertisement for *Two Against the World* at The Gaiety Picture Theatre. Despite the failure of an experiment in showing 'Animated Pictures' in 1912, the Gaiety Theatre was converted into the Gaiety Picture Theatre in 1932. It had a seating capacity of 1,100 and a foyer large enough for 800 people to wait under cover. In 1984 it closed for major alterations, reopening in June 1985 as a 3-screen complex.

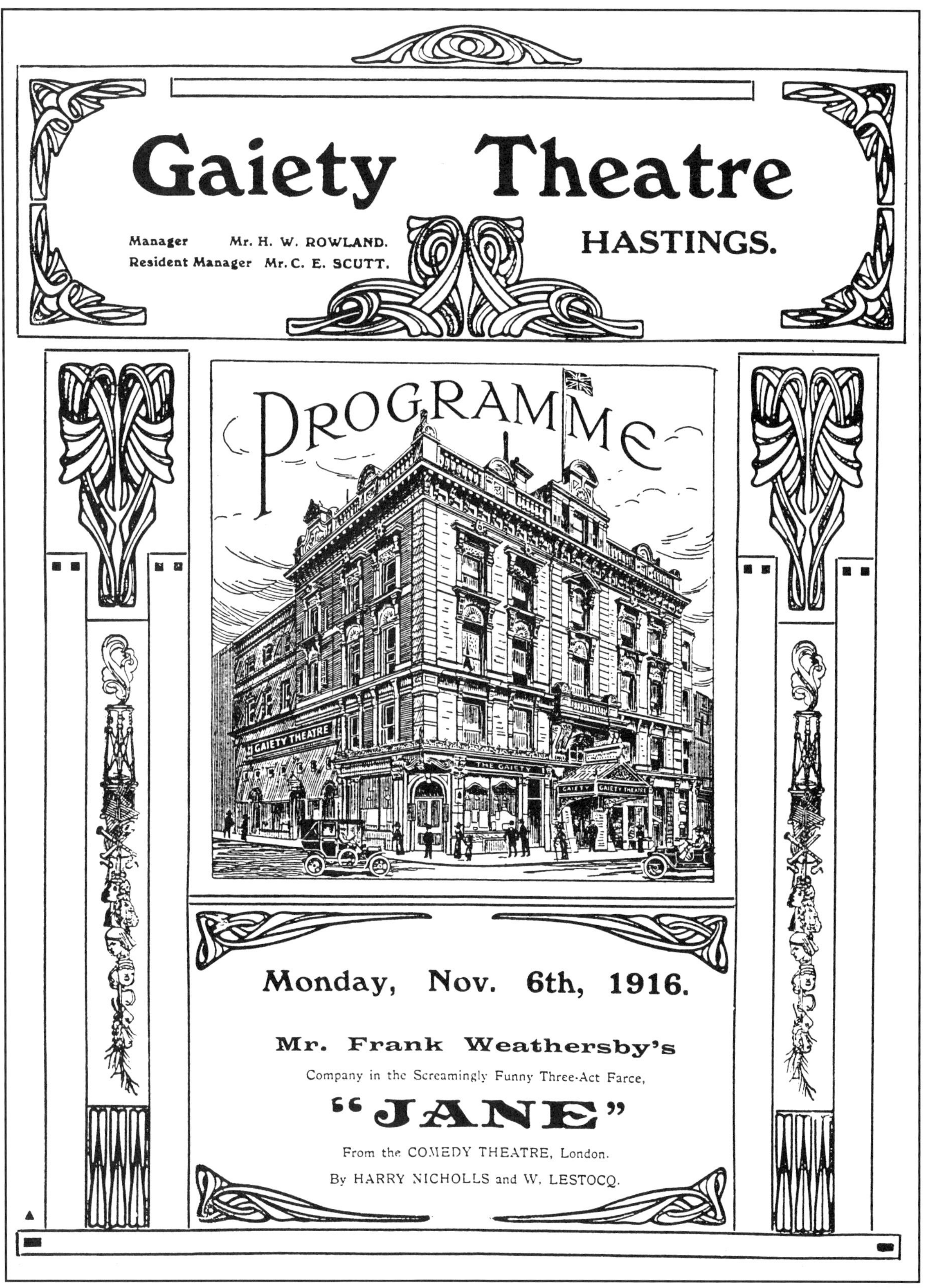

123 A programme for the Gaiety Theatre, 1916. The Gaiety's final show in 1932 was the Hastleons' production of *The Desert Song*. In the preceding 50 years, many leading stars had appeared there. When Ellen Terry played in *Captain Brassbound's Conversion* in 1907, police had to clear the way to enable her to cross Queen's Road.

124 Until well after the Second World War, the larger cinemas–the Regal, the Ritz and the Gaiety–all had their cafés and restaurants. In the years following the war there were eight cinemas in the town–Roxy, Regal, Kinema, Ritz, Penguin, Plaza (Orion), Gaiety and De Luxe.

homes, and their place in the local community was taken by caravan parks and language schools. The latter, especially, have proliferated and because of the numbers who attended them–a survey in 1995 suggested that there were 2,000 Arab students in the town–it sometimes seems that there are as many summer visitors in Hastings as there have ever been. But today's visitors do not come for the traditional British seaside holiday.

One sea-front shop still produces traditional Hastings rock, but there is not a boat or a pedalo to be hired from the beach and there are no importuning photographers on the promenade. Seaside Hastings is now largely just a memory. It is ironic that the only part of it that has survived with undiminished popularity is the Old Town area that was for so long seen as an anachronistic nuisance.

Chapter Six

900 Years of Care

THE first act of charity in Hastings was by William the Conqueror within a day or two of the battle. According to Guy of Amiens, writing *c.*1068, William's order to bury Harold on the shore near the port was carried out by a man 'partly English and partly Norman', who put a large stone over the grave. When this was done, the Duke 'distributed gifts to Christ's poor, over the buried remain'.[1]

Such charity would have been badly needed in Hastings at that time for it had been partly burned and largely wasted by the Normans. Also, the normal routines of farming and fishing had been disrupted during the long months when Harold and his forces had awaited the invasion, and so there was almost certainly much less food than usual to see everybody through the winter. Many families, too, would have lost their menfolk.

The town as a whole fairly soon recovered its prosperity but significant pockets of poverty remained endemic in the town and it was fortunate that William's example of giving was followed by many others in the succeeding centuries. In fact, the tradition of active concern for the disadvantaged became so firmly established that, by the late 19th and early 20th centuries, Hastings' record of welfare work could scarcely be matched anywhere else in the country.

125 The castle was for centuries the symbol of royal authority. It came into the ownership of the town in 1948 when Princess Elizabeth attended the ceremony at which the deeds were given into the keeping of the Corporation. At the same ceremony, the town received the gift of 215 acres of cliffland from Major Carlisle Sayer.

126 Normanhurst was the home of the Brasseys at Catsfield. Thomas Brassey, who became the 1st Earl in 1911, was closely involved in Hastings' affairs and served the town both as M.P. and mayor. His many benefactions include the Brassey Institute, which he built in 1879 to provide himself with a residence when he was mayor and to provide the town with a reference library and an assembly room.

If that sounds a wildly unlikely claim, it is probably because of the reputation that it has gained through the novel *The Ragged Trousered Philanthropist* by Robert Tressell. His powerful descriptions of the terrible poverty in the town in the first decade of the 20th century and of the cynical exploitation of its workers have been widely accepted as providing an objective picture of what life in Hastings, stigmatised as Mugsborough, was like at that time.

Tressell, however, was a propagandist and selected the details that supported his argument and his political philosophy. It is true that poverty was widespread and often extreme and that many lived in appalling conditions–my own grandmother grew up in St Leonards in the 1870s in a courtyard where a dozen or more households shared a single water source and a single lavatory–but Tressell ignored everything that was being done to combat distress and to improve the conditions.

And a great deal was being done. Surprising as it might seem, many of the advances associated with the modern welfare state were actually pioneered in Hastings. Some aged residents were receiving regular doles from local funds some 40 years before Old Age Pensions were introduced in 1908, and the equivalent of sheltered housing was being provided as early as the mid-1880s. Crêches for the 'infants of poor married women were set up at about the same time and school meals were served locally, admittedly through private charity, long before the Act of 1906 empowered local authorities to provide them.

Small payments, not to be confused with parish relief, were paid to the most needy of the unemployed decades before this idea was accepted nationally, and successful job creation schemes were in operation well before the First World War. There was also an active programme of reconditioning properties specifically with the needs of tuberculosis sufferers in mind, and Hastings was one of the pioneers, if not *the* pioneer, of the home help scheme. This was introduced and supervised by Dr. Bolton Tomson, who had inspired, and paid for, the provision of flats for tuberculosis victims.

Dr. Tomson was a committee member of the Central Aid Council, which is now the Hastings Voluntary Services organisation and which had its origins in a Mendicity Society, inaugurated in 1855 in the hope of 'abating the evil' of the beggars who had 'become so intolerable a nuisance in the town'.[2] However, this was not to be achieved through repression. Throughout the years and whatever the name it operated under, the organisation sought not merely to provide immediate relief but 'to strive always to help in a way calculated to ensure that as far as possible the need should not recur'.[3] Hence the job creation schemes.

For men, there was the Road Metal Yard enterprise. Boulders from under the Fairlight cliffs were collected by boat, taken to premises provided by the council at Rock-a-Nore and broken up for road-making. The finished product was bought by the Borough Engineer. The men were paid at the full standard rate and, because they were on piece-work, some were able to earn more than they had done at their previous jobs.

For unemployed women who had been in trades connected with dress-making, there was a toy-making project. Originally home-based, this later transferred to premises at Tackleway, and was highly successful. The soft toys were sold to outlets in Brighton and Portsmouth and to such London stores as Barkers, Pontings and Gorringes. Unfortunately, it came to an end in the First World War because of the unavailability of raw materials.

127 This picture, taken in 1925, shows the mayor and mayoress, Alderman W.J. Fellows and Mrs. A.M. Fellows, standing in front of the van that would distribute toys etc. to the children of poor families. It is believed that the mayoress's fund was the forerunner of the Mayoress's Toy Ball which later became a major social event.

ST. MATTHEW'S NEW CHURCH.

A SALE OF

Useful & Ornamental Work

WILL BE HELD ON

Thursday & Friday, Dec. 13th & 14th,

AT THE

Assembly Rooms, St. Leonards-on-Sea,

In Aid of the BUILDING FUND.

Admission first day from 2 to 5, 1s.; from 5 to 8, 6d.
Second day from 12 to 5, 1s.; from 5 to 8, 6d.

Schools and Children Half-price.

The following Ladies have kindly consented to hold Stalls :—

Mrs. ANDREWS, 1, Markwick Terrace.
Miss BLEAZBY, 10, Church Road.
Mrs. COLPOYS, 32, Kenilworth Road.
Mrs. CUMBERLEGE, Tilsworth Lodge.
Mrs. ELLIOTT, 8, Blomfield Terrace.
Mrs. NEWTON, 8, Shornden Villas.
Miss C. PARKES, Master NEWTON } Children's Stall.
Mrs. BROWNE, Miss BROPHY } Refreshment Stall.

Selections of Vocal & Instrumental Music will be given by several friends on Thursday, and on Friday by the Blind Minstrels.

Useful and Ornamental Articles, Cut Flowers and Plants, and contributions to the Refreshment Stall will be gladly received by any of the above Ladies.

128 *Left.* This programme of the sale of work in aid of St Matthew's new church dates from *c.*1880. Good works and charity fund-raising provided many leisured ladies with the illusion of leading busy and useful lives.

129 *Above.* These Boer War volunteers of 1899, photographed riding past the *Albion Hotel*, were sent off with cheers, as were the 1st Cinque Ports Rifles, who followed them from Hastings in 1900. However, there was conflict in the town between the majority jingoists and supporters of the 'Stop the War' campaign of the South Africa Conciliation Committee.

During the First World War the Central Aid Council recruited some 250 extra helpers to cope with the many extra demands that were made upon it. These included the giving of both assistance and advice to the families of servicemen and the finding of accommodation for large numbers of Belgian refugees. To provide the poor and elderly with affordable fuel, coal was bought directly from collieries and sold at just above cost price at depots manned by schoolteacher-volunteers at weekends and in the evenings.

The 5s. (25p) a week Old Age Pension soon proved totally inadequate as prices soared and the C.A.C. supplemented it for the hardest hit. Additionally, it persuaded most of those to whom it paid this supplement to keep detailed records of their spending and these records were then collated and abstracts were sent to every influential individual and organisation the C.A.C. could think of, with a letter urging concerted action to get the pension raised. It may have been purely coincidental, but a few months later the pension was increased to 7s. 6d.

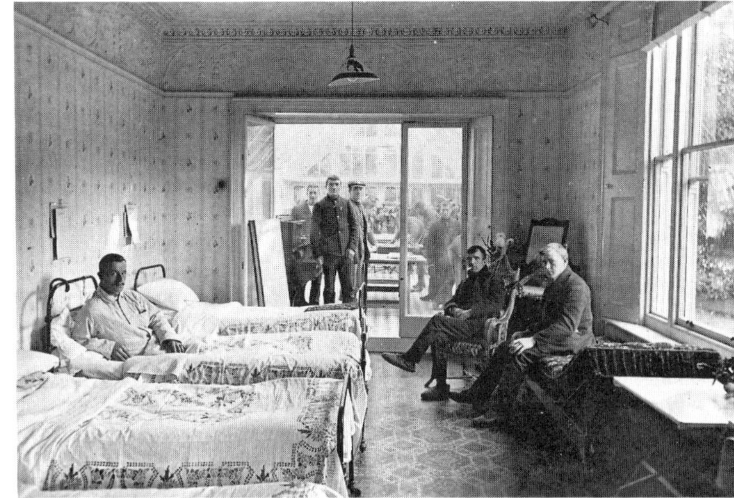

130 In the First World War the convent in Filsham Road became a hospital where the Belgian wounded were treated by VADs. A number of Belgians settled in Hastings after the war.

131 Many Belgian refugees were billeted in Hastings during the First World War. More refugees arrived during the Second World War. This group came off a tug towed into Hastings Pier by a fishing boat. Amongst them were two men whose suitcases contained 13 million francs, the working capital of the Belgian Railway Co.

132 The bulletin board, being so eagerly read here in 1915, not only gave general war news but also lists of the locals killed and wounded. During the First World War 1,300 Hastings men were killed.

133 A U-118 stranded on Hastings beach. Hastings' only experience of enemy action during the First World War was the dropping of a bomb at Cliff End by a solitary Zeppelin in 1914. Ironically, this German U-boat claimed its victims after the war when it was stranded on the beach while being towed to France in 1919. Customs men who inspected it were so badly affected by fumes from leaking batteries that one of them died.

134 During the Second World War Hastings was a possible invasion point and so in 1940 was made a restricted area. All aliens, including members of many well-liked and respected local families, were moved out of the area and all casual visitors were barred. Barbed wire, concrete anti-tank obstacles, known as dragons' teeth, and anti-aircraft guns abounded.

135 The Second World War was St Clement's Caves' finest hour. During the incessant raids, many people took nightly shelter in them and school lessons were also given here. Statistics proved the need for such a sanctuary. Bombs destroyed 463 properties in the borough and damaged another 14,818 buildings. There were 154 people killed, 260 were seriously injured and another 439 received lesser injuries.

In the Second World War the main extra demands on the C.A.C. resulted from the bombing and doodlebug raids on the town. It not only ran a Mobile Centre and took on much of the responsibility for gathering information after each 'incident', but also organised practical help for victims, in addition to giving much-needed sympathy and advice. Many thousands of pounds-worth of good quality furniture, bedding and clothing was distributed to bomb victims to replace what had been destroyed, a service that was much appreciated since official compensation was slow to come and often inadequate, being based on pre-war values rather than replacement costs–not that there was much in the shops with which to replace anything.

For all the increased general prosperity since the war, poverty remains a very real problem and the need for an umbrella organisation to co-ordinate local charity and aid work and to pioneer new initiatives remains as great as ever. It is the town's good fortune that the response is still as swift and as constructive as ever.

Nor should it be assumed, because so much was achieved by voluntary organisations and through the generosity of individuals, that corporate Hastings remained aloof from the sufferings of its old and needy. That was never the case. Right back in the Middle Ages, the ancient hospital of St Mary Magdalen, which provided care and accommodation for the destitute elderly, was apparently a town responsibility, under the

136 Sir Winston Churchill becomes a member of the Winkle Club. The council confers the Freedom of the Borough on celebrities, the fishermen make them members of the Winkle Club. Now world-renowned, the Winkle Club was formed at the turn of the century to organise a Christmas treat for Old Town children.

137 The position of the White Rock Hospital, immediately opposite the pier, was objected to for years. It was argued that it spoiled the pleasure of holiday-makers for them to be so unavoidably reminded of sickness and death. In the late 1920s, the hospital was moved to Cambridge Road and the White Rock Pavilion was erected in its place.

direct supervision of the bailiff. He had the duty of inspecting it and the right to admit 'any man or woman that hath borne hymselfe well and conveneally [respectably] and ys of good Conversacon [reputation] during theyre tyme and be Impoveryshed of theyre goods and cattells, and hath nott whearof to lyve'.[4]

The foundation of the Hospital has been put tentatively at some time in the 12th century but its position, towards present-day Bohemia, puts it a very long way from the then centre of population and raises the possibility of an earlier date, when the main part of town was still in the White Rock area. If William's encampment sprawled towards Bohemia, it is tempting to speculate that the Hospital might have originated as a treatment centre for the Norman wounded and even remained as a refuge for those too crippled to continue to support themselves.

Several hundred years later, the barons of Hastings were still revealing their charitable impulses by continuing to issue begging licences long after these had been banned, arguing that it was necessary to do so because the town 'hath byn of long tym surcharged with many and ympotent and Diseased poore people unable to labor and deprived of all other meanes to live'.[5]

At that time, Hastings was still a very small and tightly knit community but as it grew and spread beyond the Old Town valley, so the problem of poverty grew with it. By the 19th century it was not just the occasional individual who needed help but whole communities of workers and the cause of their distress was the economics of the area rather than a personal incapacity for work. Part of the problem was that Hastings did not grow in a steady and sustained fashion but in a series of frenetic spurts followed by periods of virtual stagnation. Labour was sucked into the town during the former times and then suffered badly during the latter.

In 1855, the same year in which the Mendicity Society was formed, the level of unemployment was so high and there was such widespread hardship that the Mayor started a relief fund 'to alleviate, as far as possible, the large amount of distress at present existing among the operative classes of the Borough'.[6] Within a week, over £250 had been subscribed and 650 gallons [*sic*] of bread and 300 gallons of soup distributed. Thirty years later, the scenario was repeated. The Mayor convened a public meeting 'in compliance with a requisition signed by numerous ratepayers' and the meeting, 'recognising the distress prevalent amongst the working classes in this Borough, is of opinion that a fund shall be opened for their relief'.[7]

Shortly after this Distress Fund had been set up, a letter to a local newspaper drew attention to the plight of George Monger, a man unable to work because of consumption and bronchial asthma and living in absolute destitution in Bohemia with his wife and children. There were undoubtedly many others in just as bad a state but Monger was different–he was a V.C.

He had won the medal during the Indian Mutiny when he was only 17 years old, but had had to pawn it to buy a little food for his family. To the Empire-conscious public of the time, that was more heart-stirring than the description of Monger's raggedly-clothed children cuddling up to him in a room totally devoid of furniture to try to keep him warm, and subscriptions for his relief were soon raised both locally and nationally. His former regiment, the Royal

138 Laying the foundation stone of the children's ward at Buchanan Hospital. Miss Elizabeth Mirrlees had the hospital built in 1881 to realise the wishes of her aunt, Miss Buchanan. It had six beds. Three years later, Mr. C. Eversfield provided a new site in Springfield Road and a larger hospital was built with 17 beds. The children's ward was added in 1908, thanks largely to funds provided by Mrs. Thomas Mason.

139 *Above left.* This shrimp seller had her pitch outside the *Queen's Hotel* in Harold Place. There were also flower sellers at the Memorial and every part of the town was regularly visited by itinerants pushing their barrows loaded with fish or fruit and vegtables.

140 *Above right.* In the days before social security, the man with two wooden legs was one of a good many of unfortunates who strove to get an income as best they could.

Welsh Fusiliers, sent the proceeds of a collection, even the Queen donated £5 and there was talk of a trust fund being set up. His V.C. was redeemed, his debts cleared and his family cared for. When he died on 9 August 1887, aged 47, he was buried in the town cemetery with full military honours.

Another old soldier was luckier than Monger but still ended up in the workhouse. This was William Guest, who was stationed here in 1798 and again in 1804. He married a Hastings girl and, after service in South America and in the Peninsular campaign, accompanied throughout by his wife and daughter, obtained his discharge in 1811, by which time he was master shoemaker to the regiment, and settled in Hastings to start a shoemaker's business in High Street. His wife died in 1849 and two years later he entered the Hastings Union Workhouse. He died there in 1855, aged 82.

Ending up in the Union was the dread of all the poor throughout the 19th century and, for a great many of them, the fear was realised. Despite the façade of prosperity and even elegance, poverty had become an insoluble problem and, from the middle of the century onwards, this problem worsened. Organisations such as the Mendicity Society and its successors did what they could, as did the relief committees and many charitably-minded individuals, but the problems had grown beyond them; they could alleviate but the could not cure.

As a minor illustration of the hardness of the times for many, there was always a queue outside 50, All Saints Street at the beginning of winter. Mr. Sims, an undertaker, lived there and his wife kept a room filled with blankets which she hired out for the winter at a shilling a time to those who could not afford to buy such a luxury. In the spring, they were returned and then sent to the laundry before going back into the blanket room.

Again, when the N.U.T. held a conference here early in 1909, delegates were so shocked by the numbers of children running around barefoot in the snow that they had a special collection and raised £150, which was handed over to the Hastings Education Committee, along with a further £200 from an anonymous donor, to start a new Boot Fund, the first having been set up in October the previous year. By the end of 1913, well over 2,000 pairs of new and donated boots had been distributed.

There is probably no single simple answer as to why Hastings should have been so plagued by poverty but, paradoxically, the town's early and rapid success as a seaside resort was probably a pertinent factor. As stated earlier, it grew in great spurts, each of which required a larger labour force than could be employed in the intervening periods of semi-stagnation. And agricultural distress meant that there was always a large potential labour force in the surrounding villages to compete with and even undercut the locals when there was work available, and so wages were kept permanently low.

In 1904, the editorial in a local newspaper compared the wages of skilled tradesmen in Hastings with those given in the Government's Blue Book as the average for the provinces. The writer found 'that with the exception of the smiths and cabinet makers, there is not a single trade in Hastings in which the average wages of the working-men are as high as those mentioned in the Blue Book'.[8]

In those days, it was 'no work, no pay'. Not only did outside workers face long stretches without work, because of bad weather, but, as the town came to rely more and more upon the holiday trade and at the same time started to lose its pre-eminence as a winter resort, for many this meant that work became a seasonal thing and each winter became a time of high unemployment and distress.

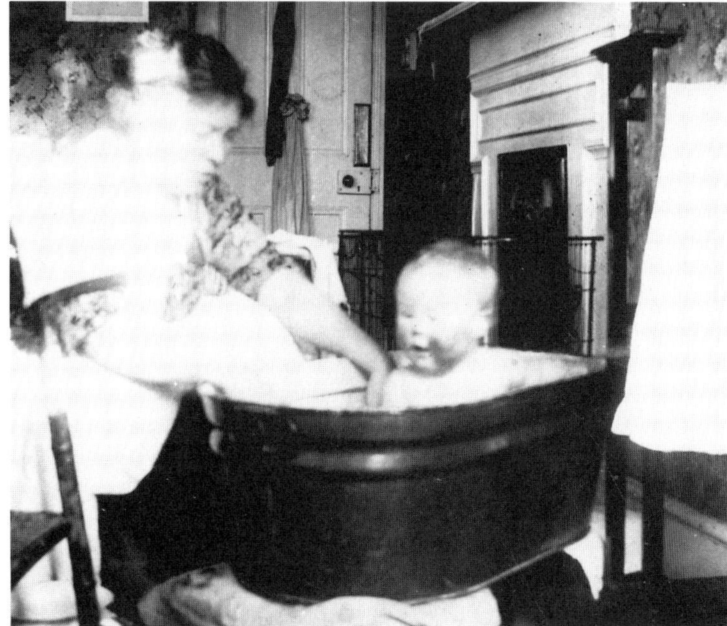

141 A middle-class nursery in St Leonards in the 1920s. To modern eyes the nursery seems to be very lacking in amenities, even if the baby is being bathed by its own nurse.

142 Bryant's outing. Although beanfeasts and annual dinners were provided by most of the larger employers, shop assistants worked very long hours for low wages and often endured very poor conditions of work.

During this time it was only the Penny Dinners and the free breakfasts and the Boot and Clothing Funds which ensured that the majority of children were kept fed and clothed. Parish relief alone was certainly not enough to achieve this. As an Old Town pastor pointed out in 1902 in an impassioned appeal on behalf of the needy, 4s. a week did not stretch very far, especially when as much as 2s. 6d. of that might be needed for rent.

Louise Santer, born in 1894, told a local history group that after her grandfather had had a stroke and could no longer work, he and her grandmother

> had to come and live with my mother and father. And all they had from the parish was half a crown [2s. 6d.] a week. And I used to come up from the village [Ore] and get that. Some people had 2 loaves of bread or a bit of flour. If you had either of them, you didn't get the money. That was the parish. I've seen poor old people cry up there when they asked if they could have a loaf of bread besides their money. Some of them only had a shilling.[9]

Free breakfasts and, in particularly necessitous cases, free lunches, were provided by the Education Committee. The Report of the School Medical Officer for 1913 revealed that 'During the winter of 1912-13 (from 4 November to 19 March) 59,333 free breakfasts were given at a cost of 1.54d. (food only) per meal, the total cost for food being £381 0s. 4d. During the year 1913, 2,041 free lunches were given at a total cost of £9 9s. 7d.'

The breakfasts were served at 8 a.m. at Ore, Old Town, Halton, Silverhill and Hollington and organised by District

Committees and voluntary helpers. There was a fixed menu. On Monday, Tuesday and Thursday each child received ½ pint oatmeal porridge, 1oz demerara sugar, a third-of-a-pint of new milk and two slices of bread and butter, dripping or jam; on Wednesday, bread and milk was served instead of porridge.

There were also Penny Dinner schemes run in various parts of the town. The Ore Penny Dinners were provided out of a voluntary fund set up in the early 1880s, and met a real need. Extra dinners were provided at Christmas and the New Year and a newspaper report of the time declared it to be 'a pleasing sight to see so many of the poorest and most ragged little ones, numbering during 4 days upwards of 460, feasting on an abundant supply of roast beef and plum-pudding'.[10] The children also received gifts of warm clothing 'many of the articles being made by servants and presented as their free-will offering to the cause'.

For the rest of the year, soup was the staple of the Penny Dinners and at Ore alone 1,000 children were fed each week at a total cost of £5. Each day the cook, a Mrs. Stretton, and her helpers boiled up 30lbs of bones and meat and half a bullock's head along with a shilling's worth of carrots, onions and potatoes and 25lbs of split peas. The second course was bread and jam–40 loaves and 7lbs of jam daily.

Far from being indignant that so many children needed this fare, the average reader of the local newspaper complacently accepted assurances that, with these dinners and the free breakfasts provided by the Education Committee, the children of Ore were really quite well fed. The same readers even felt a glow of charitable virtue when they were further reminded that the full cost of the dinners was met from private subscriptions.

As well as periodic slumps in the building trade and the problem of seasonal unemployment, a further factor in the widespread distress was the serious decline in the number of wealthier inhabitants, because these had provided so much direct and indirect employment. In the 1841 census

143 The glass hearse, which allowed the coffin to be displayed, was much in demand for the elaborate middle-class funerals in Victorian and Edwardian times.

144 A private carriage outside no. 10, The Green. Domestic service was the mainstay of a large part of the working population. In 1891, 507 men were employed as coachmen or grooms etc.; as an employment category this was topped only by labourers, who numbered 539. Of the 11,163 working women in the town, 5,898 were in domestic service.

no less than 5.35 per cent of the total male population and 11.63 per cent of the total female population were listed as being of independent means and so their importance to the local economy can scarcely be overestimated. But, generally speaking, they were not people putting down roots in the town and bringing up families. They tended to be middle-aged or elderly couples, individuals or households or parent and daughters and their numbers ceased to be replenished as Hastings lost its one-time cachet, having been overtaken by other resorts and seen to have become too urbanised and even rather vulgar as the lower-class holiday crowds grew.

What is now termed natural wastage and an actual migration from the town meant that by 1910 there were 2,000 empty properties in Hastings and a subsequent commentator recalled a significant drop in the number of private carriages to be seen on the sea front.[12] Domestic service and dressmaking having been the top two occupations for women in the 1891 census, with grooms and coachmen outnumbered only by labourers among the men, the effect of this loss of the wealthy on local job prospects was catastrophic.

It also had an effect on the funding of local relief and charity work, for there were fewer and fewer to make the large-scale donations upon which this had to a large extent depended. Certainly, the sort of retired people who later moved into Hastings were unable, and often unwilling, to replace them in this respect. As for those who flocked here, as to other resorts in the south-east, after the Second World War, earning the area the ironic soubriquet of the Costa Geriatrica, they all too often became the new poor and in need of aid themselves.

In an article in *The Planner* for November 1980, the county's Assistant Planning Officer wrote: 'The area suffers from a jobs shortage, low wage rates and an ageing population.' He could well have been summing up the history of Hastings over the previous hundred years.

Chapter Seven

'Historico-Biographies'

This book began with the Hastings of the history books, the place where the future of Britain was determined in 1066. Subsequent chapters have been of a more domestic nature, tracing the internal development of the town and detailing local events and attitudes that affected the lives and fortunes of its people.

Some of those people, though, were sufficiently remarkable in their different ways to demand special mention. A number lived lives of more than local significance and by their fame or notoriety put Hastings back in the mainstream of history. Others simply stood out from their contemporaries and neighbours, but all have stories that are worth telling. Hence this final chapter of 'Historico-Biographies', a title borrowed from T.B. Brett, who used it for his accounts of his fellow Hastingers of the 19th century.

145 Lovers' Seat, now lost following a cliff-fall, was a reminder of Hastings' most famous love story. Here the heiress, Elizabeth Boys, would wait for her forbidden lover, Captain Lamb of the revenue service, who would anchor his ship in the bay and climb up to meet her. The two eventually eloped and were married in London, not at Hollington Church in the Wood, as one version of the story has it.

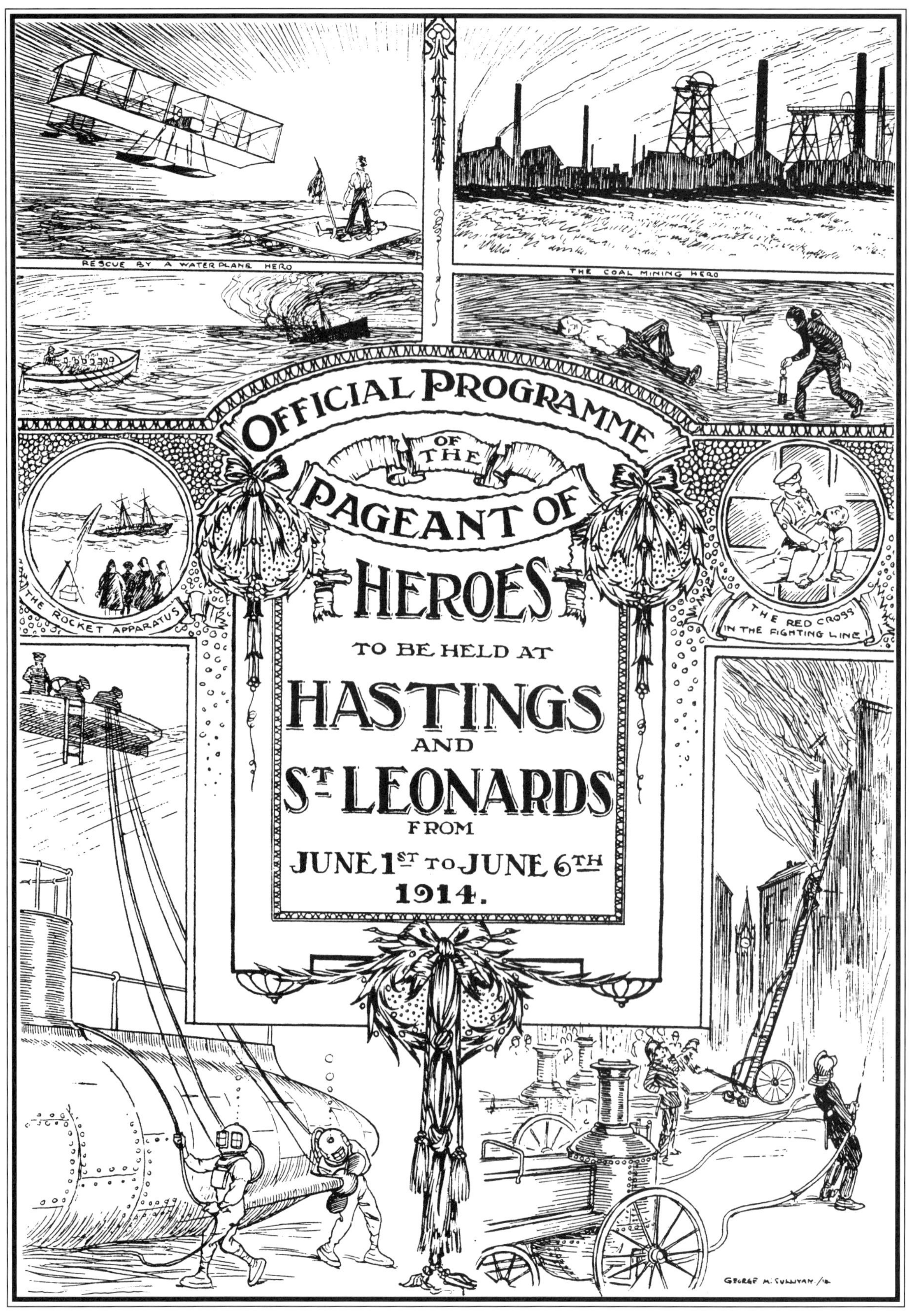
RESCUE BY A WATERPLANE HERO
THE COAL MINING HERO
OFFICIAL PROGRAMME
OF THE
PAGEANT OF
HEROES
TO BE HELD AT
HASTINGS
AND
ST LEONARDS
FROM
JUNE 1ST TO JUNE 6TH
1914.
THE ROCKET APPARATUS
THE RED CROSS IN THE FIGHTING LINE!
GEORGE M. SULLIVAN /14

Brett himself has to be included. He has already been identified as a local historian, but he was much more than that. He was one of those Victorians who seem to typify the period, multi-talented and with boundless energy, rising from poverty to middle-class comfort through unremitting hard work and an apparent ability to pack 48 hours of achievement into every 24 hours of time. He was born in 1816 and when he was ten his father, a blacksmith in George Street, died and he became the main breadwinner of the family. He had a brief spell back at school when his mother remarried in 1828 but renewed hard times soon sent him out to work again, turning his hand to anything and everything that came his way.

His abilities were as remarkable as his energy. He taught himself 'the mechanical pursuits of painting, glazing, carpentering, paper-hanging and even brick-laying' and, as he later recalled, laboured 'an average of 18 hours a day, successively and sometimes coevally at domestic work, baking, blacksmithing, drapery, post office duties, tutoring, music and private teaching; also as band master, dancing master, pedagogue, amateur architect and correspondent of local newspapers'.[1]

In 1854, he bought himself a printing press and the following year launched his own weekly newspaper, the *Hastings & St Leonards Gazette*, which he produced virtually single-handed, even doing much of the typesetting. When he died suddenly at the age of ninety, he had in his hand a treatise on vaccination that he had written and was preparing for publication. In his spare time (!) he had been a composer, producing over 100 original pieces, and had also put together a large number of manuscript volumes, now in the Hastings Public Library, recalling in remarkable detail local happenings and personalities of the 19th century.

146 *Left.* The Pageant of Heroes in 1914 included the putting up of plaques to commemorate famous residents. The organisers put up a lot of plaques but would have needed hundreds more if they had sought to honour all Hastingers or residents of Hastings with a legitimate claim to fame.

Although his memory was perhaps not quite so infallible as he liked to think, these many volumes are invaluable source material for local historians and a treasure trove of stories and characters that bring the Hastings of those days to life in a unique way. The 'facetious huckster' and the redoubtable Mrs. Piddlesden are just two of the Hastings characters who would have remained unknown but for Brett.

The former, having been a smuggler, disliked revenue men and also had a grudge against the Lord Warden of the Cinque Ports, who had ordered the confiscation of goods taken from the wreck of the *Amsterdam*, a Dutch East Indiaman wrecked on the beach at Bulverhythe. So, 'with lusty lungs and with as much irony as he could summon to his aid, [he] vended his vegetable through the new town and the old as the 'Lord Warden turn-ups' [turnips], the 'Blockhead' [Blockade] cabbages, the Amsterdam 'traitors' ['taters] etc'. He added to the amusement of his sympathetic customers by becoming 'particularly vociferous and descriptive whenever he halted–as he invariably did, at the coastguard stations and other Government offices'.[2]

Mrs. Piddlesden's story was altogether grimmer. Her husband died in 1825, a time when the resurrection men–grave robbers–were active, digging up newly-buried bodies to sell to the surgeons. She was determined that these should not have her husband and so, dressed in a tanfrock and sou'wester and armed with a lantern, she kept watch from the porch of All Saints. On the second or third night the body-snatchers arrived but she, noted as much for her courage as for being 'of masculine features and proportions', leapt out to confront and threaten them, and they, alarmed by 'her sudden appearance and, more than all, her strange gestures and gesticulations' fled for their lives.[3]

147 Biddy Stonham was famous as Biddy the Tubman and for years entertained holiday-makers with his antics off the beaches. He would entice people, preferably young ladies, into his tub and then balance on the rim and spin it around before tipping them into the sea. The men seen with him here took the collecting boxes around.

148 This drawing in the *British Workman* magazine, 1856, illustrated a story by 'Old Humphrey' (George Mogridge), a popular writer of the time who lived in Hastings–hence Old Humphrey Avenue. A great many other and better remembered writers–Thomas Carlyle, George Eliot, Lewis Carroll and Rider Haggard among them–had very close associations with the town.

149 Old Boag was a tramp who became arguably the town's best known and best loved resident. He lived in a hut by the railway line and went periodically to St Helen's Hospital for a bath and a general clean up. When he was arrested during the war for having no papers, a magistrate threw out the case, declaring that 'everybody knew Mr. Boag'.

Another of Brett's stories was of a well-to-do couple who discovered at their wedding feast that the supposed clergyman who had 'married' them at St Leonard's Church was actually a former convict just returned from transportation.

The false clergyman is something of a recurrent theme in the history of Hastings. In 1586, the Rev. Elks of St Clement's was found to have forged the Queen's order for his presentation to the living and was sentenced to be 'drawne to Tibourne and there hanged bowelled and quartred'.[4] His place as rector went to Richard Robinson, the man who had discovered the forgery.

A hundred years later, the church-wardens of All Saints were angered by a young man 'presuminge to preach, haveing not orders'.[5] He was the rector's son but that did not inhibit them from describing him as 'a malicious, disorderly, scandalous person'[6] and that condemnation was justified for the young man was Titus Oates, who was to become the most notorious and detested man in the country.

He was to lie his was into the history books with his allegations in 1678 of a Popish Plot to burn London, assassinate the king and institute a general massacre of Protestants. He created a nation-wide panic and, before his perjuries were exposed, 35 supposed conspirators had been executed on his evidence and a great many more had been imprisoned and had suffered harsh treatment.

It would be interesting to know the reactions to this in Hastings, for it had been an earlier attempt at perjury that had led to his hurried departure from the town, one step ahead of the law. He had decided that it would suit him to be master of the school that neighboured his father's rectory. First, though, he had to get ride of the incumbent,

150 The grammar school, now the William Parker Comprehensive, boasts a descent from Parker's school and claims 1619 as the date of its foundation. However, the modern grammar school opened in 1880 and from 1883 onwards occupied this building in Nelson Road. The grammar school in the castle's collegiate church survived until the sup-pression of the college in 1547.

William Parker, so he informed the magistrates that he had seen him commit an unnatural offence with one of his pupils. He then moved against the schoolmaster's father, who, as a jurat and the nephew of the former rector who had endowed the school, would have had a large say in the appointment of his son's successor. Titus deposed that he had heard him talking treason, an offence punishable by death.

However, he had over-reached himself. It was proved beyond doubt that the schoolmaster had been with the parents of some of his pupils at the time Titus claimed to have witnessed him commit the offence, and the testimony against the father was also shown to be a tissue of lies. To avoid an indictment for perjury, Titus fled from Hastings, and into the history books.

Fortunately, it was not too long before Hastings was able to wash away his shameful memory in toasts to a genuine local and national hero–General James Murray. He fought at the Battle of Quebec in 1758, taking command when Wolfe fell and then, with Lord Amherst, completed the conquest of Canada. Later he further distinguished himself as Governor of Minorca, defending the island against a year-long siege by the French and rejecting a million-pound bribe to surrender it.

As a young soldier, he had been stationed in Hastings and in 1748 had married a daughter of James Collier, who later cleared his debts and had him made a jurat, hoping that this would attach him to the town. It did. He built Beauport Park, named after the district near Quebec that his brigade had occupied, and lived there until his death in 1794, at the age of 75.

As the town grew and became fashionable, many other distinguished army and navy officers retired to Hastings or became associated with it in various ways, as did a veritable 'Who's Who' of writers and artists. Of the latter, special mention should be made of Marianne North, who had lived quietly in Hastings until the death of her father and then, in 1870, at the age of 40, set out to travel the world and to paint the exotic flowers of the countries that she visited. These paintings were later presented to Kew Gardens, where in 1882 a special gallery was opened to house them.

She was just one of a number of remarkable women connected with Hastings in the 19th and early 20th centuries, two of the most notable being the medical pioneers Dr. Elizabeth Blackwell and Dr. Sophia Jex Blake. Dr. Blackwell, who in 1849 became the first woman ever to qualify as a doctor, came to Hastings in 1869, when she was 48 years old, and lived at Rock House, Exmouth Place until her death in 1910. Sophia Jex Blake was born at 3, Croft Place in 1840.

Both of them qualified in America, where Sophia Jex Blake actually studied under Elizabeth Blackwell in New York. Later, in England, the two of them worked closely together to set up the London School of Medicine for Women, which opened in 1874, and Sophia Jex Blake became the leader of the fight in Britain to open up the medical profession to women.

Despite her world-wide fame, Dr. Blackwell was unable to overcome local prejudice sufficiently to win election to the Board of Guardians in Hastings. When she was nominated for the St Clement's Board in 1885, the editor of one of the town's newspapers commented that although she

151 Arthur Blackman ran a prosperous coal business and was founder of the Marley Co. He was mayor and a generous contributor to many causes in the town. His daughter's will set up the Isobel Blackman Foundation which has financed clinics, day centres and sheltered homes locally.

was better qualified than the other candidates, he doubted if Hastings was ready to elect a lady to such a post.[7] He was right. She came bottom of the poll.

However, more and more women of calibre were coming to the fore in Hastings at that time and eventually a Mrs. Sara Mosley succeeded where Dr. Blackwell had failed, and became a member of the Board of Guardians. Another milestone was passed in the 1890s when Mrs. J. Strickland was appointed a member of what became the Education Committee, on which she served for many years. She also became a magistrate.

She has already been mentioned in connection with the suffrage campaign and she was on the central executive of the National Union of Women's Suffrage Societies and was the signatory on behalf of the Church League for Women's Suffrage when a joint letter was sent to Asquith in 1916. Before converting to socialism–she became vice-chairman of the Hastings Labour Party–she had served on the national committee of the Women's Liberal Association.

152 Sheila Kaye-Smith, a distinctly regional novelist, was born in Dane Road, St Leonards, and grew up in the town. Another novelist who spent her childhood here was Noel Streatfeild, whose father was vicar of St Peter's.

She and another local activist, Mrs. Darent Harrison, continued to fight against discrimination after the vote had been won. In 1921, they attracted a lot of attention when they led a successful protest campaign, culminating in a petition to the Lord Chamberlain, against the proposed exclusion of women from the jury in a case of indecent assault against a 13-year-old girl.

Mrs. Darent Harrison figured in the press on several occasions and today would undoubtedly have been a media celebrity. In 1913, to prevent the bailiffs from seizing goods to be sold to defray the household tax that she refused to pay, she and a group of supporters barricaded themselves in her house and prepared for a siege, receiving food and other supplies via a basket which they lowered from an upstairs window. Unfortunately, one of the ladies left a window open when she slipped into the garden to gather flowers and the bailiffs were able to gain entry.

The calibre of the local women who fought for the vote was also demonstrated by Miss Mary Hogg and Miss Mary Tristram, who shared a home at 36, Eversfield Place. Miss Hogg was known locally as 'the paper seller', because she had a pitch at the Memorial, where, regardless of the weather, she sold the women's rights newspaper for several years. She made her own little bit of history in 1916, when she was made churchwarden of St Paul's, the first woman to hold such a post in modern times. She died in 1918.

On the outbreak of war, Miss Tristram, who had moved to Hastings because of ill-health, transferred her energies from suffragism to working for the local

153 This wintry scene was close to the studio of John Bratby, one of the many famous artists who have made their homes in Hastings. Others, including Turner, have painted here. The portrait of Whistler's mother was painted at her home in St Mary's Terrace and her grave is in Hastings cemetery.

154 Before going into business, Thomas Ross had been the last master gunner of the town battery. He had been appointed to the post in 1806 after serving for 24 years in the Royal Artillery and reaching the rank of sergeant. As master gunner his official residence was Government House on the Parade.

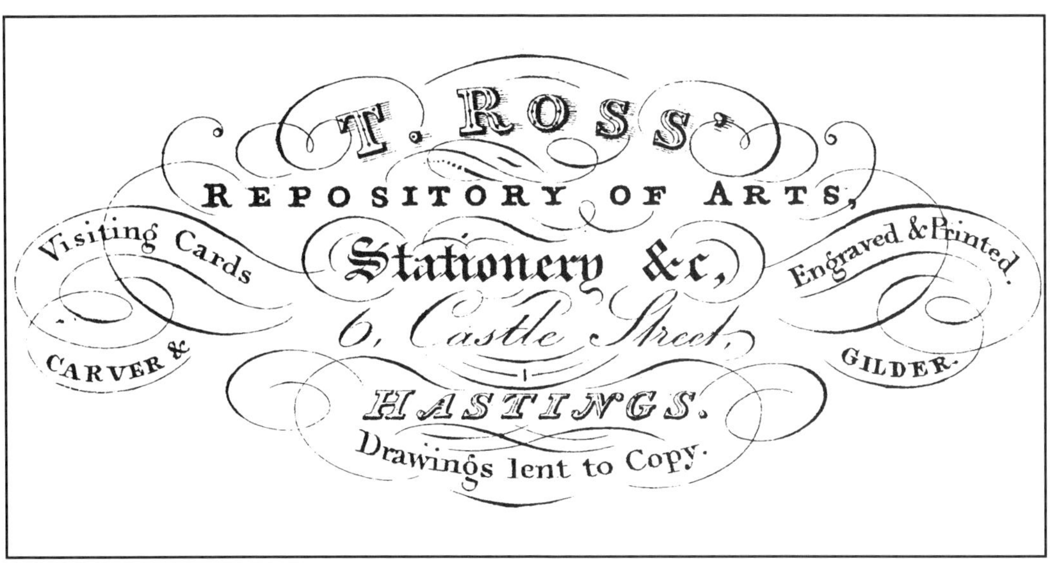

155 St Mary Star of the Sea. Coventry Patmore lived at The Mansion (Old Hastings House) from 1875-91. When his wife died in 1880, he had St Mary Star of the Sea built as a memorial to her, inviting Basil Champneys to design what 'was to be the only Catholic church in England without any bad taste in it'.

recruitment committee. After the war, she played a prominent part nationally in the foundation of the Girl Guide movement and then in the Second World War was active in Civil Defence and in the W.V.S. She died in 1949, aged 86.

Few of their local male contemporaries could match the energies and genuine achievements of these women. It is true that some of the men of roughly the same period became much more widely known, but they were mostly of a very different character; in fact, it might be more accurate to describe them as notorious rather than famous. There was, for example, a trio–George Bristow, Charles Dawson and Lewis Abbott–that might be referred to collectively as the Hastings Hoaxers, for they were responsible for two remarkable scientific frauds–the 'discovery' of Piltdown Man and the affair of the Hastings rarities. Between them, they distorted research into human origins and confused the ornithological records for half a century.

Dawson claimed that, in 1915, he and Abbott discovered the remains of humanity's most ancient ancestor in an East Sussex gravel pit. This find was estimated to be 500,000 years old and was named Eoanthropus Dawsoni in his honour but became more familiarly known as Piltdown Man. It was regarded as such an important discovery that, had Dawson not died the following year, he would quite likely have been rewarded with a knighthood.

Bristow's hoax was less spectacular but had a devastating effect on the world of ornithology. He had a taxidermy business in Silchester Road from which in the 1900s he sold stuffed and mounted specimens of many birds not previously recorded in this country but which he claimed had been shot locally.

Despite growing suspicions, it was not until the 1950s that experts were able to prove conclusively that both claims were equally fraudulent. Dawson and Abbott had salted the Piltdown gravel pit with a motley collection of bones–some possibly abstracted from the Hastings Museum, with which both men were closely connected–before making their 'discovery' and Bristow had apparently bought his birds from sailors and the like before preparing them.

For two such frauds to take place at the same time in one small town would be incredible, but when one looks at the many points of contact between the three men, not least the shared connection with the Hastings Museum, and then adds to that the fact that they had regular social meetings in the parlour behind Abbott's Grand Parade jeweller's shop, the idea of coincidence no longer becomes tenable. It becomes a fair assumption that the frauds arose from those discussions in Abbott's parlour and were planned there. It even becomes possible that there was an element of competition to see who could achieve the greatest success in fooling the experts.

If this was so then their motivations became easy to understand, which is certainly not the case with another Hastings man who, amazingly, a few years later achieved even greater fame by not merely fooling experts but by conning the entire world. This was the former Hastings Grammar School boy, Archie Belaney, who deceived everybody into accepting him as the Canadian Indian, Grey Owl, and who even had the gall to lecture in Hastings under that name without revealing his true identity.

He remains an enigma. He was born in Hastings in 1888 and is now lauded by many as a truly great Hastinger and pioneer conservationist, but a strong case can be made out for him having been just an opportunist adventurer. It could even be that his deception of the world was not a conscious fraud but that he was a pathological liar who convinced himself of the truth of his fantasy, that he was Grey Owl, the Indian.

It was as Grey Owl that he became famous in the 1920s, writing books and making lecture tours that established him as a modern St Francis of the Indians; as stated above, he even lectured in Hastings without his real identity being discovered. It is as Grey Owl that he is remembered today, the plaque to his memory in Hastings Country Park recording that he had become alarmed by 'the wanton slaughter of wildlife' and so began a personal crusade for recognition of 'the natural brotherhood between man and animals'.

He attracted, and continues to attract, hero-worship. When his reputation temporarily slumped following his death in 1938 and the revelation of his fraud, a Hastings admirer complained bitterly that 'To belittle such a unique, as well as infinitely kind, gentle and courageous personality is unworthy of English-speaking people. His like will not soon pass this way again'.[8]

Unfortunately, one of the few certainties about Grey Owl, or Archie Belaney, is that he definitely did not deserve that character reference. Before becoming world famous as a conservationist, he had been renowned in his part of Canada for his profanity, his drunken and riotous behaviour, his violence and an over-readiness to use a knife. His reputation was such that at one stage the Forestry Service refused to employ him as a Fire Ranger, which had been his usual job out of the hunting season.

His record with women was particularly bad. He married an Indian girl in 1910 but soon deserted her and left her to bring up their daughter alone and unsupported. His own comment on this was allegedly, 'When I discovered I didn't like marriage, I dropped it like a hot potato'. Not that this stopped him from contracting a number of other bigamous marriages and relationships. In 1914, he walked out on another Indian girl when she became pregnant, joined the Army and then, whilst convalescing in Hastings after being wounded in the foot, 'married 'a local girl, Connie Holmes. But as soon as he was told that he could be returned to Canada for discharge, he threw his wedding ring into the sea and left immediately. So it went on.

As for the 'natural brotherhood between man and animals', he made use of strychnine in his hunting and obtained the beaver kits, upon which his St Francis image became founded, by trapping out of season. It was the Indian girl with whom he was then living who persuaded him not to sell the kits, as he had originally intended. Instead, he put them on show and, as a result, was asked to give a talk. He accepted this invitation and a new career, and a legend, was born.

The genuineness or otherwise of his conversion is really no longer an issue. Nor is his character. He caught the imaginations of millions and as Grey Owl inspired many to respond to the need to protect wildlife and the wilderness. He may not have been the noblest Hastinger of them all, but he must rank as one of the most noteworthy.

In their very different ways, two other Hastingers, one of whom acquired posthumous fame while the other worked hard at being notorious, showed something of the same retreat from reality that was such a feature of Grey Owl's life. The first of these was Robert Noonan, better remembered as the socialist author Robert Tressell, under which name he lived and worked in Hastings in the early 1900s. His novel, *The Ragged Trousered Philanthropist*, inspired by his experiences in Hastings, is now accepted as 'the classic novel of British socialism'. For some reason, he obscured the details of his origins and early life. His biographer found it difficult to penetrate his various aliases and described him as 'a somewhat enigmatic figure, someone who seemed to re-invent himself at each new turning point in his short life'.[9]

The second celebrity, Aleister Crowley, who made his home in Hastings for several years before his death in 1947, was also a man of secrets but his secrets were deliberately created and publicised to enhance his reputation and ensure his notoriety. He was an occultist who lived out his fantasy life in the public eye, identifying himself as 'the Great Beast of Revelations' and delighted that the press labelled him 'the wickedest man in the world'.

But if Grey Owl, Crowley and, to some extent, Tressell each had his own dream world, then John Logie Baird, who lived in Hastings briefly in the 1920s, created a world of dreams for everybody. He came to Hastings for the good of his health in 1923 and the following year, after experiments in his lodgings in Linton Crescent and in premises rented at 8, Queen's Arcade, achieved the world's first successful transmission of television pictures. Amazingly, he did that with apparatus created from a tea chest and a biscuit tin, with scanning discs cut from cardboard and lenses taken from bicycle lamps. He also used darning needles and driftwood from the beach. The total cost of his apparatus was 7s. 6d.

So, in 1066 the future of Britain was determined at Hastings and 858 years later Hastings was the birthplace of a new age for the entire world. Nevertheless, since Hastings and 1066 are so much an automatic pairing, it seems appropriate to go back to the era of the battle for the final one of these 'historico-biographies'. It is actually a double entry, of husband and wife. The husband was in Hastings only briefly and the wife not at all. Even so, their entry is justified for not only are they in the history books in connection with the town but they remind us that the

156 Netherwood was the unlikely seeming last home of the notorious Aleister Crowley, who before the war had been thrown out of Italy after allegations that he had conducted devil worshipping ceremonies that had involved sexual depravity and possibly even human sacrifice.

people in the history books were once living human beings.

Humphrey of Tilleul was highly regarded by William for his prowess as a knight and so the Conqueror put into his hands 'the custody of the Castle of Hastings from the first day of its building'.[10] Humphrey, though, had a wife and she was not pleased to be left languishing in Normandy but had no intention of coming to England to live in what was no more than an armed camp and, in any case, shrank from the prospect of the Channel crossing. So she sent Humphrey an ultimatum. Either he returned to her in Normandy or he could accept the responsibility should she fill the empty space in their marriage bed with someone else. For Humphrey the call of love outweighed the demands of duty. He and his brother-in-law, who had received a similar letter, immediately resigned their commands and sailed home to save their marriages. Or, as the disapproving Ordericus Vitalis, from whom we get the story, put it: 'They returned obsequiously to their lascivious wives in Normandy'.[11]

References

Chapter I

1. Cousins, Henry, *Hastings of Bygone Days and the Present* (1921), p.12.
2. Brodribb, G., 'Beauport Park', *Current Archaeology* No.77 (1981), p.177.
3. Lower, M.A., 'Landing of William the Conqueror', *Sussex Archaeological Collections* (hereafter SAC), Vol.2 (1849), p.56.
4. Thiery, A., *Norman Conquest of England* (1825), quoted by Lower, *SAC*, Vol.2 (1849), p.55.
5. Whitelock, Dorothy (ed.), *English Historical Documents*, 2nd Edn. (1979), Vol.1, p.247.
6. Beresford, M., *New Towns of the Middle Ages* (1967), p.201.
7. Salzman, L.F. (ed.), *Victoria History of the County of Sussex*, Vol.9 (1937), p.23.
8. Moss, W.G., *History and Antiquities of the Town and Port of Hastings* (1824), p.8.
9. Dawson, Charles, *History of Hastings Castle* (hereafter *HHC*), (1909), Vol.1, p.40fn.
10. Dawson, Charles, *HHC*, Vol.1, p.33.
11. Dawson, Charles, *HHC*, Vol.2, p.499.
12. Dawson, Charles, *HHC*, Vol.2, p.501.

Chapter II

1. Dawson, Charles, *HHC*, Vol.1, p.160fn.
2. Dawson, Charles, *HHC*, Vol.1, p.121.
3. Diplock, W., *Hastings Past and Present* (1855), p.26.
4. Melling, Henry, 'Sketches in the Year 1831', *The Camera*, No.1.
5. Dawson, Charles, *HHC*, Vol.2, p.256.
6. Diplock, W., *Hastings Past and Present* (1855), Appendix XL, note 43.
7. Fleet, C., *Glimpses of our Sussex Ancestors*, 2nd ed. (1882), p.73.
8. Fleet, C., *Glimpses of our Sussex Ancestors*, 2nd ed. (1882), p.73.
9. Baines, J. Manwaring, *Historic Hastings* (1955), p.254.
10. Banks, J., *Reminiscences of Smugglers and Smuggling* (*c.*1873).
11. Brett, T.B., 'Histories' (unpublished), Vol.1, p.102.
12. Cousins, Henry, *History of Bygone Days and the Present* (1921), p.150.
13. Baines, J. Manwaring, *Historic Hastings* (1955), p.227.

Chapter III

1. Dawson, Charles, *HHC* (1909), Vol.1, p.96.
2. Cooper, William Durrant and Ross, Thomas, 'Notices of Hastings', *SAC* (1862), Vol.14, p.75.
3. *ibid.*
4. *Hastings and St Leonards News*, 16 July 1852..
5. *Hastings and St Leonards Chronicle*, 18 June 1884.
6. Brett, T.B., 'Histories' (unpublished), Vol.1, p.100.
7. Moss, W.G., *History and Antiquities of the Town and Port of Hastings* (1824), p.158.
8. *Hastings and St Leonards Chronicle*, 5 November 1884.
9. *ibid.*, 12 November 1884.
10. Sawyer, F.E., 'Sussex Folk-lore and Customs', *SAC* (1883), Vol.33, p.247.
11. *Hastings and St Leonards News*, 27 July 1855.
12. *ibid.*, 1 August 1856.

Chapter IV

1. Belt, A. (ed.), *Hastings: A Survey of Times Past and Present* (1937), p.156.
2. Pennant, Thomas, *Journey From London to the Isle of Wight* (1801).
3. Dymond, T.S., *Memoirs of a Mayor of Hastings* (1928), p.39.
4. Baines, J. Manwaring, *Historic Hastings* (1955), p.64.
5. North, Marianne, *Recollections of a Happy Life* (1893), Vol.1, p.34.
6. Moss, W.G., *History and Antiquities of the Town and Port of Hastings* (1824), p.124.

Chapter V

1. *Hastings and St Leonards News*, 21 April 1865.
2. *Guide to All the Watering and Sea-Bathing Places* (1803), pp.218-9.
3. *Hastings Pocket Guide 1828.*
4. Walton, John K., *The English Seaside Resort* (1983), p.55.
5. *General Development Plan of Hastings and St Leonards 1930.*
6. *Hastings and St Leonards Chronicle*, 24 April 1864.
7. Hastings Modern History Workshop, *Hastings Voices* (1982), p.36.
8. Anderson and Swinglehurst, *Victorian and Edwardian Seaside* (1978), p.71.
9. Diplock, W., *Hastings Past and Present* (1855), p.317.
10. *ibid.*, p.318.
11. Belt, A. (ed.), *Hastings: A Survey of Times Past and Present* (1937), p.201.
12. *Hastings Pocket Guide 1828.*
13. Elleray, D.R., *Hastings: A Pictorial History* (1979), Introduction.

Chapter VI

1. Dawson, Charles, *HHC*, Vol.2, p.568.
2. *Hastings and St Leonards Chronicle*, 17 January 1855.
3. Elford, L. Harvey, *Sixty Year of Voluntary Service* (1951), p.6.
4. Baines, J. Mainwaring, *Historic Hastings* (1955), p.106.
5. Cooper, William Durrant and Ross, Thomas, 'Notices of Hastings', *SAC* (1862), Vol.14, p.105.
6. *Hastings and St Leonards Chronicle*, 21 February 1855.
7. *Hastings and St Leonards Observer*, 4 February 1885.
8. *Hastings and St Leonards Observer*, 23 January 1904.
9. Hastings Modern History Workshop, *Hastings Voices* (1982), p.15.
10. *Hastings and St Leonards Chronicle*, 7 January 1885.
11. Dymond, T.S., *Memoirs of a Mayor of Hastings* (1928), p.95.

Chapter VII

1. *Hastings and St Leonards Observer*, 7 April 1906.
2. Brett, T.B., 'Histories' (unpublished), Vol.1, p.56.
3. *ibid.*, p.86.
4. Horsfield, T.W., *History, Antiquities and Topography of the County of Sussex* (ed. of 1974), p.453.
5. Baines, J. Manwaring, *Historic Hastings* (1955), p.116.
6. *ibid.*, p.117.
7. *Hastings and St Leonards Chronicle*, 8 April 1885.
8. *Hastings and St Leonards Observer*, 30 April 1938.
9. Ball, Fred, *One of the Damned* (1973), blurb.
10. Dawson, Charles, *HHC* (1909), Vol.1, p.17.

Index

References to illustrations are given in **bold**.

BREEDS'

BOTTLED BEERS

ON SALE AT

THEATRE BARS.

QUEEN'S HOTEL, HASTING

SUNDAY AFTERNOON CONCERT TE

Are served in the Lounge, Price 1/-

On Saturday and Sunday Evenings AFTER DINNER CONCER

Are held at 8-15. OPEN TO THE PUBLIC.

Table d'Hote Dinner 5/- Table d'Hote Luncheor

An up-to-date Restaurant adjoins the Hotel where Meals are served at Popular Pr

The Queen's is the leading & best Hotel and is renowned for excellent cooking & accommo

En Pension terms can be arranged from 3½ guineas a week.

E. HAROLD PAULL Mana

THE GRAND RESTAURANT,

Opposite Hastings Pier.

HIGH-CLASS. FULLY LICENSED.

TABLE D'HOTE MEALS AS UNDER

Luncheon	-	12-30, to 2-30	-	1/9
Dinner	-	6-30 ,, 8- 0	-	2/9
Supper	-	9- 0 ,, 10-0	-	1/6

LIGHT REFRESHMENTS and DAINTY TEAS a Speciality.

ORCHESTRA, 4 till 5-30 and 7 till 9. (Sundays included).

Proprietors - R. M. KEY, Ltd.

GAIETY THEATRE, HASTINGS

Manager - Mr. H. W. ROWLAND,

Resident Manager - Mr. C. E. SCUTT.

TELEPHONE No 517

Monday, Nov. 6th. Six Nights at 7-

Matinee—Saturday at 2-30.

Mr. Frank Weathersby's

Company in the Screamingly Funny Three-Act Farce,

"JANE"

From the COMEDY THEATRE, London.

By HARRY NICHOLLS and W. LESTOCQ.

PROGRAMME OF MUSIC.

March	"Irish Guards"	H
Overture ...	"Silver Cross"	He
Selection	"Push and Go" ...	Da
Waltz ...	"Molly Dear"	De

GOD SAVE THE KING.

The right of alteration is reserved.

Musical Director Mr. THOS. HILTON.

Furniture by BRYANT & SON, 44 and 46, Queen's Road, Hastings.

Refreshment Department under the Direct Control of the Manage
A Special Feature—Fresh Chocolates every week.

ALL PRICES INCLUDE WAR TAX.

Reserved Seats—Boxes, £2 6s., £1 14s. 6d., and £1 3s. Circle, 4/3. Dress Circle, 3/3. Orchestra Stalls, 3/3. Circle (Centre), 2/2.

Unreserved Seats—Pit Stalls, 2/2. Upper Circle (Sides) Pit, 1/2. Gallery, 7d. Gallery not open at Matinees.

N. Half-price to Gallery. Children in arms not admitted

BOX OFFICE OPEN DAILY FROM 11 TILL 9

Ordinary Doors at 6-45 Commence at 7-15

For the convenience of St. Leonards Residents, Seats may be booked at KI LIBRARIES, 48, King's Road, and 77, Bohemia Road.

N.B. Cheques should be made payable to "Hastings Theatre Co."

'FLEXIFORM' NATURAL CURVE CORSETS.

Regd. design No. 608943.

FITTED WITH

"EMPIRELLA"

WASHABLE, UNBREAKABLE and RUSTPROOF.

MOST COMFORTABLE AND BEST FITTING CORSETS EVER PRODUCED.

ALL PRICES 4/11½ to 29/6

N. & E. MARTIN, 10, LONDON RD., ST. LEONARDS.

Ladies' Outfitters and Corset Specialists.

FOR BOOKINGS OF

The Royal Concert Hall

(Seating Accommodation 1,000), and

The Masonic Hall

(Seating Accommodation 300).

Also for Small Halls and Rooms for Private Meetings, etc.,

APPLY TO—

KING BROS., Stationers, Printers, and Concert Agents,

2, Queen's Road, Hastings.

48, King's Road, & 77, Bohemia Road, St. Leonards.

A Delightful SKIN BALM for all Seasons

"ELFIN" TOILET LOTION,

Protects against Sun, Wind and Dust. 6d and 1/- per Bottle.

One of the Finest TOOTH PASTES is

GOODMAN'S DENTAL CREAM

Regular 1/- size for 10d.

F. W. GOODMAN, The Park Pharmacy, HASTINGS.

(Opposite Park Gates).

ASSEMBLY RO

68, Norman Road, St. L

DANCI

Wednesdays & Saturdays

WHIST DRI

Mondays & Thursdays,

Admission, 6d.

Private Lessons in Dancing by

Mrs. TOLHURST, at above